the smart approach to®
small space
LIVING

CREATIVE
HOMEOWNER®

the smart approach to®

small space

LIVING

Susan Boyle Hillstrom

CREATIVE HOMEOWNER®, Upper Saddle River, New Jersey

COPYRIGHT © 2007

CRE▲TIVE
HOMEOWNER®

A Division of Federal Marketing Corp.
Upper Saddle River, NJ

THE SMART APPROACH TO® SMALL SPACE LIVING

SENIOR EDITOR	Kathie Robitz
SENIOR GRAPHIC DESIGN COORDINATOR	Glee Barre
PHOTO EDITOR	Stan Sudol
EDITORIAL ASSISTANT	Jennifer Calvert
INDEXER	Schroeder Indexing Services
COVER DESIGN	Glee Barre
FRONT COVER PHOTOGRAPHY	Tria Giovan
INSIDE FRONT COVER PHOTOGRAPHY	(top) Tria Giovan; (bottom) Mark Lohman
BACK COVER PHOTOGRAPHY	(top) Karyn Millet; (middle) Bjorg Magnea; (bottom) Olson Photography LLC
INSIDE BACK COVER PHOTOGRAPHY	(top) Bob Greenspan, stylist: Susan Andrews; (bottom) Mark Lohman

CREATIVE HOMEOWNER

VICE PRESIDENT AND PUBLISHER	Timothy O. Bakke
PRODUCTION DIRECTOR	Kimberly H. Vivas
ART DIRECTOR	David Geer
MANAGING EDITOR	Fran J. Donegan

Current Printing (last digit)
10 9 8 7 6 5 4 3 2 1

The Smart Approach to® Small Space Living
Library of Congress Control Number: 2006935503
ISBN10: 1-58011-345-1
ISBN-13: 978-1-58011-345-8

CREATIVE HOMEOWNER®
A Division of Federal Marketing Corp.
24 Park Way
Upper Saddle River, NJ 07458
www.creativehomeowner.com

acknowledgments

As usual it was a pleasure to work with my editor Kathie Robitz, who is smart, funny, and long-suffering. Also as usual my husband Roger Hillstrom was helpful and patient.

Special thanks also to designers Patricia Gaylor and Lucianna Samu for their creative ideas. And photography editor Stan Sudol for some great pictures.

contents

introduction

Let's be clear about something right away: there is nothing wrong with *small.* In fact, have you noticed that the soaring ceilings, mega-living rooms, gargantuan kitchens, and palatial baths in many new houses feel *too large?* These spaces seem to lack human scale, dwarfing the furniture and even the people in them at times.

The Smart Approach to® Small Space Living, therefore, will not tell you that bigger is better. Nor does it suggest that you embark on an expensive remodeling to enlarge your house. It does, however, offer you some good advice for making those space-challenged places feel—and live—larger by making a few easy, economical alterations, using color and lighting creatively, and selecting furniture that is in keeping with the scale of the space. Along with these smart tips, *The Smart Approach to® Small Space Living* encourages you to embrace the dimensions of your small home. With a little care and attention, a tiny bedroom can be intimate and restful; a pint-size powder room can be drop-dead gorgeous; and a modest kitchen can produce great meals.

first things first

THE BASICS OF DESIGN   GETTING STARTED   DESIGN WORKBOOK

Form follows function, as interior designers, architects, and other design professionals are fond of saying. This phrase, made famous in the early 1900s by American architect Louis Henri Sullivan (his actual words: "form ever follows function") is especially apt when you apply it to the outfitting of small living spaces—a modest-size house or apartment or just a particularly small room.

When you haven't got a lot of square footage with which to work and you can't add on, you need to be careful and intentional about making the most of it. Happily, if you focus first on how you want to use the room, other considerations, such as layout, furniture, colors, and accessories, will fall easily into place. Simply put, once the function is established, all else is likely to follow.

LEFT
In this living room, symmetrical balance and color harmony create order while the oil painting adds interest.

the basics of design

Y ou probably know people who can combine furniture, colors, fabrics, and accessories with ease and somehow make a room look wonderful. "How did you do that?" you may wonder. And usually these gifted people answer, "I don't know; it all just came together. Intuition, I guess."

Lots of people decorate their homes guided by this kind of design intuition. Sometimes it works—sometimes it doesn't. If you don't have a gift for intuitive, sure-handed decorating, don't worry. The basic principles will succeed where intuition fails.

You probably already know quite a lot about the elements of design—color, pattern, texture, and form, to name just a few— and may have had great success in choosing and combining these elements. You know what you like, what colors speak to you, what textures please your eye and blend with the character and architecture of your home. But to make the most of your small spaces, focus first on the principles of design—scale, proportion, line, balance, harmony, and rhythm.

LEFT
Designers often look to nature for inspiration. This pretty shell helped establish the beachy theme in the room at right.

RIGHT
Color, fabric, and texture cooperate here to produce an appealing space with a relaxed seaside theme. L-shape banquette seating on two sides of the dining table make the most of the narrow room. A wide doorway makes the kitchen feel roomier, too.

smart steps
the road rules

■ Step 1 FIND SCALE AND PROPORTION

In the world of interior design, scale refers to the size of an object compared with the size of everything else in the room, including other objects, people, or the space in which it is located. Proportion refers to the relationship of parts or objects to one another based on size. Proper scale is achieved when all of the parts are proportionately correct relative to one another as well as to the whole. The principles of scale and pro-portion pertain to all items in a room, from architectural elements, such as windows, doors, and moldings, to furniture, color, window treatments, accessories, and even patterns and prints. All of these objects should be scaled to the size of the room and proportional to the other items in the room.

When you are furnishing and equipping your small space, pay attention to how items you choose relate to the size of the room (scale) and to each other (proportion) in terms of size. For example, a grand piano would be out of scale in your small living room, and a recliner that is too big in relation to the other furniture will diminish everything around it and make other pieces look puny. Conversely, a delicate coffee table

would fade into oblivion placed in front of a chunky, oversize sofa.

Generally, you'll have no trouble recognizing that a certain element is too little or too much for your space, but it takes training to achieve good proportion. Develop your abilities by reading decorating magazines and design books. Study photographs of rooms that have been put together by professionals, and try to understand why they work so well. Above all, practice. You'll soon develop a discerning eye.

Step 2 DEFINE LINE

Line defines space. Two-dimensional space consists of flat surfaces, such as walls, floors, and ceilings, which

LEFT
In a small city apartment with few windows, the living room, dining area, and kitchen occupy a single open space. To make it feel as light and open as possible, the designer chose simple furniture and a palette of pale colors. Banquettes lining two walls in the dining area are great space savers.

ABOVE
An emphasis on vertical line, sleek and simple cabinets, and a monochromatic color scheme work together to create the illusion of height and space in a tiny galley kitchen.

BELOW
Without the design principles of scale, proportion, and balance, the varied objects on the wall and sideboard in this dining room would have looked like a jumbled mess. The mirror also helps to anchor all of the elements.

OPPOSITE
Tiny windows carved into a living-room wall allow glimpses of the outdoors without compromising privacy indoors. Had their placement not been governed by balance, a basic principle of interior design, the room might have felt chaotic. But because the windows are all the same size and are positioned an equal distance from each other, and from the fireplace, they have an eye-pleasing symmetry.

are formed by intersecting lines. Adding depth, or volume, to a flat surface creates the three-dimensional space we experience when we enter a room. Lines do more than define space, however—they also suggest various qualities.

Vertical lines imply strength and dignity, and an emphasis on verticality creates a formal atmosphere in a room. A classical column, for example, always appears strong and stately. Vertical lines also add height and offset the horizontal lines of most furniture.

Horizontal lines, as exemplified by beds, tables of various sizes, cabinets, and other built-ins, suggest relaxation and security.

Diagonal lines, such as gable roofs or the railings of interior staircases, express motion, transition, and change; they attract attention and lead the eye.

Curved lines, such as you see in a winding path, a round table, or the arms of a comfy overstuffed chair, suggest freedom, softness, and sensuality.

When creating the design for your small space, look for ways to incorporate a variety of lines. The architectural shape of most rooms is strongly rectilinear, and much furniture is rectilinear as well. To relieve the sharpness of rectangles and squares and make the room livelier and more interesting, throw in a few curves or diagonals with windows, furniture, moldings, or accessories. To make a room look taller, incorporate some vertical lines; for width, use horizontal lines.

Step 3 CREATE BALANCE

Another important spatial concept, balance refers to the equilibrium among objects in a room. A well-balanced room gives careful consideration to the placement of objects according to their visual weight. With good balance, relationships between the objects will seem natural and comfortable to the eye, resulting in a blissful state called visual equilibrium. The room will exude a sense of repose and a feeling of completeness.

Two framed pictures hanging side by side will please the eye if they are of approximately equal weight and size, while the pairing of two pictures of unequal size will immediately look wrong and disturb the eye. The same goes for furniture, whether large or small; in a balanced room the pieces will be distributed evenly, not delegated to only one part of the room.

There are two approaches to balance—symmetrical

smart tip   CHECKING REFERENCES

Ask professionals for at least three references; more is better. When you talk to former clients, get creative with your questions. According to N'ann Harp of Smart Consumer Services, a Burnside, North Carolina, consumer-assistance organization that specializes in homeowner-contractor relationships, "Homeowners need to ask a lot of questions. Not just, 'Would you hire this person again?' Take the time to delve into details of the project with previous customers. The complaints we most often hear are about the project going over-time and over-budget, and finishing details being left undone.

So it's particularly important to ask about these issues."
Here are some of the questions Harp recommends asking:

■ Could you communicate well with the designer or contractor?
■ Was he or she respectful of your ideas?
■ Did the professional show up on time?
■ Was the job completed on time? On budget?
■ Did the designer or contractor stay in touch throughout the project?
■ Would you use this person again without hesitation?

and asymmetrical. Symmetry is defined as the same arrangement of parts, objects, or forms on both sides of an imagined or real center line, a mirror-image sort of approach. By nature, it is formal. Picture a fireplace with a chair and sconce on either side of it. To make the symmetry pleasing to the eye, the chairs and sconces must be identical or at least of equal weight and size. If the arrangement is even slightly off, it will be jarring and distracting.

Asymmetrical balance uses different objects of the same visual weight to create equilibrium. Picture a grouping of tall, slender candlesticks on one side of a mantelpiece and a short, wide vase on the other side. As long as the scale is correct, this grouping is in balance. Asymmetry can be every bit as pleasing to the eye as symmetry and, because it is informal, often suits the casual tone of contemporary spaces.

Step 4   ESTABLISH HARMONY AND RHYTHM

These two principles concern creating patterns in space. Harmony results when elements work together

OPPOSITE
One way to make a small room feel larger is to eliminate clutter and other discordant elements. Here, with nothing to distract the eye from traveling freely through the space, a sort of visual serenity is achieved. The room's white color scheme enhances the spatial flow.

RIGHT
With its emphasis on clean line and minimal ornamentation, modern design makes any space feel larger and more open. This clutter-free bedroom is a case in point.

to form a visually pleasing cohesiveness. It's achieved when all of the elements relate to one another; that is, when everything coordinates within one color scheme or design motif.

Honoring the principle of harmony does not require that colors and patterns match in every way—that kind of repetition is boring and lifeless. But to create harmony in a room's decor, these elements must connect in some way, such as by colors that relate closely or contrast subtly. You can combine several patterns or prints, as well; try mixing florals, stripes, and checks, for example, provided that they are linked by scale, motif, or color palette.

In decorating, rhythm is often referred to as the continuity or lack thereof that creates stimulating design, specifically through repetition of line, form, color, pattern, or texture. If harmony pulls a room together, rhythm moves the eye around, following the colors, textures, and shapes that flow from one part of the space to another. The color palette may remain the same, but emphasizing a particular color in one area

and downplaying it in another will create rhythm and bring space to life.

Rhythm is an effective design tool for small spaces, says interior designer Patricia Gaylor of Little Falls, New Jersey. "To make a small room appear larger and more open, it needs to be visually uncluttered so that the eye travels around the space without stopping, without being distracted. Objects that distract the eye stop the trail of vision, disrupting the initial reaction to the room.

"It may sound a little hokey," says Gaylor, "but it's true. When your eye can move peacefully across a space, you experience a sort of visual serenity."

What mistakes would stop the eye on its serene tour of the room? "The use of too many colors," says Gaylor, "or colors that contrast too dramatically. Even the use of light and dark woods in the same room can be disruptive; the wood pieces should be in roughly the same tonal family. An ultra-large piece of furniture that knocks the whole room out of scale is a big distraction, too."

getting started

Armed with an understanding of the fundamentals of interior design, you can proceed with confidence to tackle the small spaces in your life.

But, says Patricia Gaylor, before you start working with scale, balance, or rhythm, be clear about how the space will actually function. If it's a living room, for example, will you use it for entertaining? For TV watching? For quiet pursuits such as bill paying, reading, or homework? For all of these activities? If it's a kitchen, will you limit its use to food preparation, or will you eat meals there, invite guests to gather, set up a home office? Give careful thought to these questions, and encourage the input of family members as well.

Next, ask yourself, what will make this room livable and workable for me and my family? What elements must the room contain? Apply these questions to any small room that is challenging you—living room, bedroom, kitchen, even a bath.

If you want to conduct all of the activities mentioned above in the living room, you will need comfortable chairs, maybe a couch, a TV, a desk, a coffee table or side tables to hold drinks and snacks, and a quiet corner for reading. It may be difficult to fit all of these into a small living room. In that case, you might want to limit the activities that will take place there and find another spot, perhaps the kitchen, for bill paying or designate a section of the bedroom for reading.

Here's where scale and proportion come into play. Once you know that to fulfill its purpose the room should contain specific pieces of furniture, you need to check that these items will be in proportion to each other and to the physical dimensions of the room. "This is the time for logic," says Patricia Gaylor. "You can't get emotional yet. You've got to measure the room, measure the furniture, and be certain that it will all fit." One way to do this, she says, is with an on-line home-design software program that can produce a floor plan in scale, then turn it into 3-D picture. Do-it-yourself scale drawings with movable cutouts for furniture and appliances are also useful tools. "Moving around the scaled furniture pieces lets you see what will fit.

"It's hard to size for a room," Gaylor

LEFT
With no extra rooms to spare, the owners of this house combined home office and guest room. The ceiling-high shelves hold files, family photos, and collectibles, and the built-in desk preserves floor space.

OPPOSITE
A round table and scaled-down sideboard suit the less-than-generous dimensions of this dining room.

admits. "Unless you've got a trained eye, you can't rely on your own powers of visualization to tell you how a piece you love in a showroom will fit at home. Once in a while clients will call me after they have bought something large—for instance, a huge leather sectional—that was on sale. Good price but way too big. Then they want me to make it work, which I can't always do." So if a soft, fluffy oversize sofa or a luxurious king-size bed is on your wish list, she advises, first make sure that it will fit through the door and, second, that it won't overwhelm the room—before you make a purchase.

Interior designer Tracey Stephens, ASID, of Montclair, New Jersey, agrees that scale drawings are important. "I've found that I get many more ideas looking at the floor plan than I do looking at the physical space," she says. "It allows me to think outside the box. If I'm looking only at the room itself, I tend to get stuck."

After you've been logical, almost mathematical, about your small space, you can get emotional, says Gaylor. This is the time to create a wish list of furniture pieces—appropriately sized, of course—and start fantasizing about the colors, fabrics, textures, and accessories you love.

Working with a Professional

If the prospect of outfitting your small space seems daunting, you might want to hire a design professional to get you started. You can turn the entire project over to a pro or, if your budget is limited, sign up for a consultation only, which may be enough to point you in the right direction. Generally speaking, design professionals are willing to work on a consulting basis. Patricia Gaylor says she charges from $110 to $125 per hour, plus travel time, for such consultations. She estimates that helping a client make the most of a small living space, complete with drawings and specifications for furniture, would take her about five hours. "For an initial investment of about $500, the clients are well on their way to a great new room," she says.

Occasionally Gaylor does hourly consultations via e-mail or regular mail. "I have certain requirements for that," she says. "I ask clients to send me measurements and photographs of the room; a description of the proposed use for the room; existing or new pieces they want to use; some sort of direction for style; storage issues, if any; and about how much they want to spend for furnishings and so forth."

Another way to get help that won't break your budget may be through a home center, furniture store, or the furniture department of a large department store. Some of these establishments employ decorators and in-store consultants who help customers deal with decorating dilemmas. Going this route will probably not provide you with an in-depth design experience, but it may be all you need.

If you are fairly confident about your own abilities to meet your small-space challenge, taking inspiration from photographs, touring designer showhouses, or visiting helpful sites on the Internet may be sufficient.

None of the small-space strategies recommended here involves adding physical space or changing the basic footprint of your home, alterations that would probably require the services of an architect. In Chapter Two, "Playing with Space," beginning on page 28, you'll learn about a variety of ways to rethink an existing layout to maximize its usefulness. Some of those projects are simple; a carpenter or general handyman can probably

OPPOSITE
A glass-top coffee table helps create an illusion of space in a small apartment living area. Round shapes are easier to walk around, too.

BELOW
Bright white paint on the wainscoting and good lighting rescues a long, narrow hallway from claustrophobia.

smart tip

DECORATORS' SHOWHOUSES

To sharpen your design savvy and absorb ideas you can use at home, take some time to wander through the rooms in a decorators' showhouse in your area. The ticket you buy will benefit a local charity, and you'll get to see the elements and principles of design at work as interpreted by a dozen or so local designers, architects, and landscape designers. Some of the rooms may be over the top, but never mind—you'll find inspiration somewhere.

To find a showhouse in your area, contact a local American Society of Interior Designers (ASID) chapter or call the home-and-garden editor of your area newspaper.

handle the work. If you have the skills and experience, you might take on those jobs yourself. Installing new windows, cabinets or appliances? In-store or showroom installers often do that kind of work. If you're adding new kitchen or bath fixtures, call your plumber. New lighting system? Call your electrician. Need to simplify your home—and your life—before you tackle that small room? Call a space planner. These people, as their titles suggest, are experts at organizing certain types of interior space; most of them are specialists in planning and building in storage, outfitting closets, and helping clients get free of clutter.

If you're afraid to move ahead without still more professional advice, factor fees into your budget and start looking for a design professional.

An interior designer, architectural designer, or spatial consultant might be the person you need. Anyone with a degree in interior design has been trained in space planning; construction, including creating working drawings and specifications; ergonomics; lighting; design for the elderly and disabled; and of course, surface treatments such as furnishings, paint, fabric, wallcoverings, and other materials. Because they are familiar with home furnishings and have access to showrooms, interior designers can also expand the decorative possibilities for your space.

The letters "ASID" after a name indicates membership in the American Society of Interior Designers, a national

trade association. "ASID members," says Tracey Stephens, "have had professional training and a certain amount of practical on-the-job experience and are likely to be as familiar with space planning and construction as they are with surface treatments."

Is your kitchen the undersized room that's presenting challenges? If so, you may want to contact a certified kitchen designer. CKDs are trained and certified specifically in kitchen design by the National Kitchen & Bath Association (NKBA). They can create functional layouts and advise you about products—such as small-scale appliances—that are designed for compact spaces.

Certified Bath Designers (CBDs) are also trained and certified by the NKBA. These specialists can help you choose the layout and fixtures that will make the most of a small bath.

smart tip

A LOW CEILING

Give it the illusion of height by selecting pieces of furniture that sit low to the ground; then hang paintings and other artwork higher than normal, choosing shapes that are more vertical than horizontal. Hanging curtains as high as possible also creates an illusion of height.

smart tip YOUR OWN DESIGN NOTEBOOK

Whether you're upgrading one small room or an entire space-challenged house, keeping a file of ideas, measurements, drawings, and plans will be a great help.

Use a loose-leaf binder, and begin by recording your analysis of the existing space and your ideas and goals for it. List the best and worst features of the room, calling attention to important aspects such as the view and the times of day that the room gets the most sun. Note the location of doors, windows, closets, and staircases. Jot down the activities you expect the room to accommodate, along with storage you may require. As your project moves along you can add paint chips, fabric and wallpaper samples, and pictures from magazines that illustrate looks you love. Don't forget to include style numbers and dimensions, too, when you're recording favorite furniture pieces.

design workbook
ONE LONG, OPEN SPACE

loft living

This former commercial loft was updated for family living. Every inch of space counts. (See before photo, left.)

long division

Modular orange wall panels hide the kitchen. Furniture and a rug define the living area. (See also center left.)

stylish solutions

The "dining room/library" can accommodate a dinner party or a quiet, solitary read. To save space, bookcases were built into the walls. They delineate the area without enclosing it.

light levels

The chandelier adds intimacy and glamour. Its proportions suit the space. (See also far left.)

modern moves

The spare lines of the furniture enhance the sense of free-flowing space. (See also left.)

playing with space

NEW ARRANGEMENTS   ADJOINING AREAS   DESIGN WORKBOOK

Guided by logic and the basic principles of good design, you can usually make the most of any small house or limited space. The right furniture and the judicious use of color and light can also help transform a boxy room or layout into comfortable space that lives larger than its actual square footage. However, there may be times when rearranging existing interior space might be the best solution or the most practical alternative to expanding your house. If for one reason or another—your budget, local zoning ordinances, no room to expand—you cannot add on to your house, there may be opportunities for interior changes that can expand the physical dimensions of your space-challenged rooms. In this chapter you'll find ideas for expanding the look and feel of your house by rethinking or reconfiguring what you already have.

LEFT
Here's a great way to expand—take down the top half of a wall and frame the new opening with stylish columns.

new arrangements

Because some of the ideas in this chapter are simple and straightforward home-improvement projects, you may want to tackle them yourself, especially if your budget is tight. However, unless you are a skilled and experienced do-it-yourselfer, you'd be well advised to hire professional help for the more complex jobs, such as tearing down an interior wall or creating an opening for a new window.

"For most projects that rearrange interior space, I would not recommend a do-it-yourself approach," says interior designer Tracey Stephens. "For example, widening an existing doorway requires a new header to support the weight of the wall above. Any qualified contractor could do it, but a structural alteration such as this may be beyond a homeowner's expertise. And it's important to do it right; a mistake could cause big problems." (Before you decide to take on any space-rearranging projects, take the DIY quiz on page 33.)

Tear Down a Wall

Knocking down an interior wall—or even a portion of one—can do wonders for a small room, opening up space, bringing in light, improving circulation patterns, and enhancing function and sociability. Perhaps a small, little-used dining room shares a wall with your undersized living area. Tearing down that wall might nicely solve your space problem, and with a little creative furniture rearrangement you can use part of the room for dining but

LEFT
Load-bearing walls can be removed if you compensate. Here, an open wall between the kitchen and living room is possible thanks to a boxed support beam and posts.

OPPOSITE
A raised ceiling in a once-industrial loft opens up space; exposed ductwork is now part of the design.

LEFT
With a wall removed, this kitchen and dining room are one. A new peninsula counter defines the space and offers a mini-eating area.

OPPOSITE
Here, both natural and artificial Illumination rescue a tiny hallway in a New York apartment from claustrophobia.

devote the majority of the square footage to living space.

If your kitchen and living room share a wall, you've got an ideal situation for expansion. Remove the dividing wall, and you've created a congenial open-plan kitchen that can become the heart of your home. And your living room will instantly become more casual, feel larger, and make an important connection to activities that go on in the kitchen.

To safeguard your food-preparation zone and keep family and friends from strolling through while you're cooking, build in an island to define space. You don't have to invest in an expensive piece of new cabinetry to create a work-area boundary. A freestanding kitchen island will do the job nicely. Flea markets and antique stores abound with pieces that can be used as islands—a handsome sideboard, the bottom part of a Hoosier cabinet, a refectory table, and more.

Another way to open up space is to remove only the top half of a dividing wall. The half-wall that's left will clearly demarcate different areas of function, and the opening above it will bring in light and extend sightlines, making both spaces feel much larger. With a small investment of time and money, you will have connected the two spaces but maintained the distinction between them.

In my own house, where a long hall runs from entry to back door, my husband and I cut out part of the wall between the hall and the adjoining living room. The interior window that resulted brought light into the formerly dark hall and made it feel more roomy. It also created an interesting architectural feature. Because we left a half-wall standing in the cutout, we still had wall space in the living room for furniture placement. A similar example can be seen in the photograph on page 28.

should you do it yourself?

I f you're thinking of handling the task on your own, take a few minutes to evaluate your skills and abilities by answering the following questions.

- Do you enjoy physical work?

- Do you have the time to do the job? Will it matter if the project remains unfinished for a period of time? (When gauging the time it will take, you should probably double it.)

- Are you persistent? Will the project get finished?

- Do you have the necessary skills—and tools—to do the job, including the expertise to install appliances, cabinets, and other equipment?

- Will you need assistance? If so, do you have access to a skilled labor pool?

- Are you familiar with local building codes and permit requirements?

- Have you considered safety issues? Some jobs—electricity, roofing—have serious consequences if performed incorrectly.

- Can you get the materials you'll need? Who will be your supplier?

- Are you hoping to save money by doing it yourself? Will you, in fact, save once you factor in the cost of materials, your time, tools, or helpers you may have to pay, and mistakes you may have to correct?

- What will you do if something goes wrong and you can't correct it? (Most contractors are wary about stepping in to save a botched D-I-Y job.)

None of these are projects that you can toss off in a couple of hours. In the first place, you don't want to mess with load-bearing walls, and it's not easy to identify them, especially if your house is older and has undergone previous renovations. Secondly, if the section you want to remove is lengthy, you may need to build in supports whether the wall is load bearing or not. And even if your goal is to alter only a small portion of a wall, you could still run into trouble. As you swing the sledgehammer, you may unearth plumbing, wiring, or other mechanical equipment lurking in the wall. If any of these have to be rerouted, it will significantly complicate the work. Unfortunately, you can't always tell by looking what surprises may await you. Forewarned is forearmed—unless you are skilled and experienced at home-improvement projects, you probably should turn these jobs over to a professional.

Beef Up the Windows

Replacing a window is a fairly easy project that a skilled do-it-yourselfer can handle in a day. No doubt, you'll get a more energy-efficient window and perhaps also a better-looking one; but unless it's also larger than the one you are replacing, a new window is not going to make a difference in opening up or brightening your small room.

However, if you enlarge existing windows or put in one or two new ones, you'll definitely see the space in a new light. Keep in mind, though, that both of these projects involve breaking through an exterior wall, a project not recommended for non-professionals. For this job, you need a general contractor or the in-house installer from the store or home center that sold you the windows.

smart steps
think before acting

Step 1 DO YOUR HOMEWORK

Before you invest any money in the window project, invest some time looking at books, magazines, and catalogs—or drive by houses that are similar to yours architecturally—and study the windows. Your new window should look as good from the outside as it does on the inside, so you'll need to be sure it's in keeping with the overall architecture of your house and harmonious in style, scale, and proportion with existing windows. Windows are available in a large array of styles today, so it will be no problem to match new ones to existing ones. While you're at it, you may want to add some design interest with a round-top window, clerestory, or transom.

Step 2 PLACE WINDOWS PROPERLY

Give some thought to exterior placement, too. Windows are generally positioned very intentionally so that they create a pattern on the exterior of a house. If you change either the window style or the pattern of placement, you may inadvertently create an exterior eyesore.

Give some thought, also, to interior placement of a new window. What sort of view will you be capturing? If you'll be looking at part of a garden or a stand of trees or a distant meadow, go for it. But if you'll be facing the neighbor's ramshackle garage or an ugly blank wall, maybe you should regroup. A new window that must be curtained or screened to block an ugly view won't bring in much light and might not be worth the expense.

Step 3 ASSESS THE LIGHT

What kind of light will spill through the new window? A southern exposure offers the most sunlight, but heat build-up could be a problem, especially in summer, unless the window is covered. West-facing windows also attract heat on summer afternoons. Northern light is cool, not as bright, and eastern exposure is bright in the morning, which may be ideal for a bedroom, bath, or kitchen.

Fresh air is also a consideration. If possible, position

ABOVE
If there is a pleasant view on the other side of a solid door, think about replacing it with a glass one. This simple and relatively economical remodeling project will extend sightlines and usher in daylight, making the interior space look and feel larger.

OPPOSITE TOP
Originally, this modest-sized enclosed porch had drafty windows, which made the space unusable except in warm weather. The owners replaced the old units with new, energy-efficient ones, taking care to match the original architecture. The result is an extra sitting room that can be enjoyed year-round.

OPPOSITE BOTTOM
If you plan to add new windows to a solid wall, be sure to have the proper support in place. Here, a structural beam spans the width of the wall between the glass doors and the clerestory windows above them.

the new windows so that they coordinate with existing ones to create cross-currents of fresh air and cool breezes on warm days.

Tracey Stephens suggests a couple of other ways to illuminate a small space. "As long as you're intending to break through an exterior wall," she says, "why not replace a standard window with a glass door?" This project will capture even more light and extend sight-lines by providing outdoor views. If the door leads out to a garden or patio, so much the better.

Stephens is also keen on skylights. "Anytime you can see up to the sky, you feel as if you have more space," she says. But beware, unless you chose a high-quality product and have it put in by an experienced installer, you're asking for leaks. It's usually not the skylight itself that leaks but the metal flashing around it. In fact, an improperly flashed skylight practically guarantees leaks—rain spilling down a sloping roof easily infiltrates the frame of the skylight and drips into the house. Unless you have successfully put in skylights before, turn this project over to a professional. Stores that sell skylights often employ in-house installers who are familiar with the project and the product and guarantee the work.

Whatever the size or shape of the windows you add, keep energy savings in mind. According to the Environmental Protection Agency, the average household spends more than 40 percent of its annual energy costs on heating and cooling. To pare down these costs, look for windows with the Energy Star label, a national symbol for energy efficiency.

smart tip PORCHES AND DECKS

Adding a front porch or rear deck to your home extends usable living space outdoors during warm weather. And because these alfresco areas make possible so many activities—sipping morning coffee or afternoon iced tea, reading, sunbathing, grilling a perfect steak, eating, or even sleeping under the stars—they are valuable additions, especially when they are attached to a house with a space-challenged interior.

But porches and decks also extend apparent space, making the rooms that look out onto them feel larger and more open. And they perform this service all year long. Even when cold weather prevents you from sitting outside, you can still see outside. It's that sightline thing again—whenever you can see from one area into another, the space around you feels larger, even if the area at which you're looking is a porch or deck.

ABOVE

When windows don't seem to capture enough sunshine to brighten small rooms, consider installing a skylight. A large unit in this building bathes a tiny kitchen with abundant light.

TOP RIGHT

In some cases, new windows bring in space-enhancing sunshine but frame views you'd rather not see. The owners solved that problem in this small room by using a gauzy window treatment that lets in light and hides the view at the same time. The round window high in the gable adds architectural distinction and light.

RIGHT

A French door or any door with a glass panel can brighten a small and stuffy entry hall.

adjoining areas

Are you convinced that there is no possible way to enlarge your small room? Before you dismiss the idea of expansion entirely, take a look at the areas that surround the room in question. Is there a closet, a hallway, or even a part of an adjoining room that you would be willing to sacrifice to the cause?

Older houses, with their small rooms, odd little hallways, and plethora of tiny closets, readily lend themselves to this type of project. One of these spaces can often be "borrowed" to expand a second-floor bath or create a master suite.

The same kind of situation may present itself in your own home. Perhaps a dining room adjoins your living room; you may not want to give up all of the dining space, but by moving the adjoining wall a few feet you can gain a bigger living room and still end up with an adequate space for dining. In another scenario, a large foyer, hallway, or roomy coat closet might be annexed to make a living area or family room bigger. (These space-stretching strategies can also work wonders with kitchens, which are discussed in Chapter 4, beginning on page 44.)

Linda and Jack McKernan of Oneonta, New York, enlarged their narrow living room by annexing most of the space of a long hallway that paralleled the living room as it meandered from the front to the back of the house. Leaving the first few feet of the hallway wall intact to preserve a sense of entry, the couple knocked down the rest of the wall to add about 60 square feet to the living room. "It's not a lot of space," says Jack, "but it was just enough to make the living room more usable and sociable." Linda agrees that it was a good move. "It's easier now to entertain," she says, "because the extra space allows a more inviting arrangement of furniture."

"Backing in" to a closet or hallway that shares a wall with your living area or family room may yield valuable storage space. This project will not make the room any larger but it will create a niche for a bookcase, an entertainment center, or a bar, thus preserving precious floor area.

Raise the Ceiling

In many new houses, ceilings are reaching for the sky. According to a recent survey of residential builders conducted by the National Association of Home Builders (NAHB), 42 percent reported that first-floor ceilings in their new homes rose to at least 9 feet; and 15 percent said that their homes boasted ceilings higher than 9 feet. In a 2005 American Institute of Architects (AIA) survey, 51 percent of the architects interviewed said that they

OPPOSITE
Before remodeling, this living room sat under a double-height ceiling that dwarfed the furniture and was too tall for the room's less-than-generous dimensions. The designer's solution was to construct a loft that holds an upper-level seating area and lowers the living room ceiling to a proportional, cozy height.

RIGHT
One effective way to open up a small, crowded kitchen is to remove the wall that separates it from an adjoining room. Here, an extra-long work island takes the place of the old wall, and the kitchen flows directly into the dining space, creating a sociable, open-plan layout that encourages family and guests to become part of meal preparation. The granite-topped island holds a cooktop and plenty of counter space and can serve as a buffet area.

routinely specified high ceilings, two-story-high entries, and vaulted ceilings to add volume to their designs.

The picture is very different in most houses, especially older ones where ceilings may be only 7 feet high. A low ceiling can be cozy or cramped, depending on your point of view. In the living spaces of one-story houses built after World War II, such as ranches or split-levels—or in second-floor bedrooms of two-story houses—raising the ceiling is very doable, and the results can be dramatic. With rafters and the roofline exposed, a cathedral ceiling can soar above the once-cramped room, making it feel significantly larger.

This is another project that is not recommended for do-it-yourselfers. The demolition and basic carpentry may be easy enough for a skilled homeowner, but some knowledge of structural matters is necessary for the next part: adequately bracing and supporting the roof. Tim Carter who writes a nationally syndicated newspaper column called "Ask the Builder," puts it this way, "If you don't adequately brace the roof, you can cause serious structural damage. In the worst case your roof will collapse on top of you. This process can happen over a period of years, months, or even seconds, depending on how your house is built."

Making the high-ceilinged room livable may also require expertise in design and building techniques. Rooms with cathedral ceilings are notoriously difficult to heat and cool—and you could find yourself in an altered space that looks spectacular but feels less than homey. (And it may not yield actual extra living room.) Condensation that builds up in the insulated cavity space can lead to wood rot and mold, compromising the structural integrity of the roof and the air quality of the room. To avoid hot and cold spots and unwanted moisture, you'll need to add the right kind and amount of insulation and provide adequate ventilation.

Cautions notwithstanding, creating a cathedral ceiling can be a worthwhile project in a room of moderate size, but in

BELOW
Under its original 7½-foot-high ceiling, this living room in a 1950s ranch felt cramped and confining. To make it live larger, the homeowners raised the ceiling and installed new windows on either side of the fireplace.

OPPOSITE
You can also maximize the flow of space and light by widening a doorway. In this enlarged opening, glass doors enhance openness but can be closed for privacy or noise control.

a very small room, a cathedral ceiling would be out of proportion to the other dimensions of the room, feeling more like a vault or tunnel than an airy, open space. To compensate, says spatial consultant Ann Grasso, "Even if you open the ceiling to the ridge, you can box the beams, which tames the volume. Or you can raise the ceiling only part of the way so that it doesn't soar right up to the ridge; the flat ceiling that results is a useful surface from which to hang lighting fixtures, too."

"A 7-foot-high ceiling is pretty low," Grasso admits, "but it was standard in many American houses from the 1940s through the 1980s. Sometimes we deal with it by slightly dropping the ceiling around the perimeter of the room, then "vaulting" the center by trimming it with and egg-and-dart motif and decorating it or painting it a different color, often a light blue, which makes it look even higher."

Redesigning Doorways

Another simple strategy for making spaces appear larger and flow better is to widen—or remove—existing doorways. A wider doorway between two rooms not only means more light and a better spatial flow but also strengthens the connection between rooms. Another advantage—new sightlines. Whenever you can gaze from one room into another, your eye "extends" the space.

Tracey Stephens has used this technique to great effect in kitchen renovations, but it would provide benefits anywhere space is tight. "Existing doors usually measure 30 to 36 inches wide," says Stephens. "I like to enlarge the opening to about 5 feet, then trim it with moldings that are appropriate to the rest of the rooms. It creates a much better flow."

Closing off one or more doorways is another option. In some houses—usually older ones—several doors open into a single room, interfering with the flow of space and using up wall space that could be used for furniture, especially additional storage pieces. Fortunately, some of these doors are unnecessary. If that is your case, you can eliminate them and the problems they cause. You can remove a door and its trim and then cover the opening with new wallboard. Depending on the width of the opening, you may have to install a wall stud. However, even this seemingly simple job is not for all do-it-yourselfers, says Tracey Stephens. "Unless you're really skilled at plastering, sanding, and painting, you'll be able to see where the door was."

Another tip from Stephens, "Sometimes you can't do without a door. But if the swing of a standard door into a room is causing a problem, you can replace it with a pocket door, which takes up less floor space."

design workbook
NEW STYLE FROM OLD BONES

transformed within

When the walls came down in this three-story New York town house, a maze of tiny rooms became an up-to-date open plan, with the kitchen and living room, left, sharing opposite ends of the ground floor. The old fireplace, beams, and wood flooring remain to sustain the period look.

"expanded" by light

The almost all-white color scheme used thoughout visually creates the sense of one large space.

retaining character

Removing a wall on the second floor opened up space in the tiny sitting room, left, but the original posts still stand, defining the room's boundaries and honoring the building's architectural history. Slender windows, original to the house, magnify vertical space.

design workbook
NEW USE FOR AN OLD GARAGE

no-nonsense materials

Looking to add space on a shoe-string? Why not convert your garage into a fabulous family room and home office? Simple, low-cost materials, such as a concrete floor and concrete-block hearth, are clean and contemporary.

chrome and glass

A large glass table and chrome chairs, top left, keep the look modern and sleek. The door stays open in nice weather to capture light and breezes.

architectural accent

Seating clusters around the concrete-block hearth, far left—the room's striking focal point.

snack time

A mini kitchen, left, handles snacks. Small drawer units on casters fit under the freestanding island.

LEFT
Enlarged by removing a wall, this kitchen now opens to the living area. A new center island supplies additional work space.

3

kitchens

REARRANGE THE KITCHEN YOU HAVE   MAKING THE BEST OF IT
DESIGN WORKBOOK

During the last several decades the appeal of the large kitchen has spread far and wide. Magazines, design books, and home-improvement TV shows proclaim the glories of these mega-rooms with their fancy, over-sized appliances, double and triple sinks—and the square footage necessary to accommodate all of these high-ticket items.

It's nice to dream, but that sort of luxury is beyond the budgets and space allotments many people possess. Happily, bigger is not always better, and generous dimensions and acres of counter space don't necessarily provide what is really necessary in a kitchen. So if you are not able to build a new kitchen or add a significant amount of space to the existing one, don't worry. There are many other ways to make your compact room function well, look good, and feel more spacious than it really is.

rearrange the kitchen you have

Short of undertaking major remodeling projects to enlarge a small kitchen, there are probably some interior changes you can make that will give you a bit more floor area or work space—and in the kitchen every square foot counts.

BELOW

A new and expanded kitchen was not in the homeowners' budget, so they made cosmetic changes that brightened this room and made it a tad more efficient. For example, they painted the old dark wood cabinets white and replaced some solid doors with ones that have glass fronts. They also removed the doors from a small cabinet over the range to create a display area. A vintage table with leaves, found at a garage sale, serves as an island.

OPPOSITE

Structural or financial restrictions may preclude removing an entire wall, but you could create a pass-through that will, at least partially, open up the kitchen. Removing a wall cabinet made way for this opening, which brings in light from the family room.

smart steps
how to get more

Step 1 OPEN IT UP

A claustrophobic kitchen, hemmed in on every side by walls, feels smaller than it actually is. If you can't add square footage, you may be able to make a big difference in the room's size and openness by tearing down an interior wall.

In many floor plans, the kitchen is adjacent to a breakfast area, dining room, or living room. If that's the situation in your house, removing a wall may solve your limited-space problem beautifully by creating an open-plan kitchen that shares space with another room of the house. The square footage you have annexed will give you a more sociable, welcoming kitchen and allow you to expand your food-preparation area.

Then, to establish boundaries and keep household traffic out of the work zone, you could add an island, which will clearly define the kitchen proper and augment your counter area. If your existing kitchen layout is crowded, with appliances and work centers jammed too close together, you could move, say, the sink to the island or invest in a new island cooktop, thereby freeing up space elsewhere in the room for badly needed work counters. If there's space, select an extra-deep island so that the far side of it can serve as a snack counter, serving area, or gathering place. Add a couple of stools, and let guests sit, sip wine, and talk to you while you cook.

In these days of huge, welcoming kitchens, it is assumed that everyone likes help fixing a meal and enjoys talking to people at the same time. But the truth is that not everyone likes it. If you and the other cooks in your household prefer a little solitude, think about enlarging your kitchen by opening up one-half of a wall instead of a full one. You could top off the half-wall that remains with a multi-purpose pass-through/snack counter. This alteration will bring in light, create a better spatial flow, lengthen your sightlines, and make you feel less confined—and at the same time provide a clear boundary. You'll be able to see family and friends and chat with them as much as you like, but they will in fact be in another room.

You can also add the illusion of space by carving out a small pass-through or interestingly shaped interior window or by simply widening the doorway between the kitchen and the next room. Trim these new openings with moldings that match the existing architecture, and they'll look as if they've always been there.

In some older houses, particularly ranch-style designs from the 1940s, '50s, and '60s, cabinets were hung above a peninsula counter that separated the kitchen from a breakfast area or a dining room. If you've got a situation like this, no wonder your kitchen feels cramped. Getting rid of those cabinets will instantly brighten the room and make it feel larger. If you need the offending cabinets for storage, hang them a foot or so higher so that they allow you to see into the next room.

Adding, enlarging, or relocating windows can also help. In one of her small-kitchen projects, certified kitchen designer (CKD) Lori Jo Krengel of Kitchens by Krengel in St. Paul, Minnesota, removed a standard window and replaced it with a row of transom units high on the wall above the original opening. "We gained critical wall space for storage cabinets without losing light," she says. "I'm a great believer in not expanding a kitchen when a good design will satisfy most needs."

Step 2 BORROW SPACE

Before you resign yourself to the current square footage of your kitchen, cast a critical eye at such adjacent spaces as pantries, mudrooms, closets, and hallways. Are any of them expendable? If so, annex them for the kitchen. Borrowing even a few square feet can make a big difference. Sometimes even inches count, says Lori Jo Krengel. In one kitchen, she removed the wall between a kitchen and a hallway. "It didn't add up to much in terms of square footage," she says, "but it created an illusion of width and allowed for a shelf to be built on the new kitchen wall, which freed up valuable space elsewhere."

If a large mudroom or laundry center adjoins your kitchen, you may be able to "borrow" a portion of it for use as kitchen space. Is there a closet in the kitchen, or one that backs up to a kitchen wall? Gain some precious floor space by turning the former closet into a pantry to beef up your storage, or use it as a niche for the refrigerator. "A recessed refrigerator gives the wall a smooth look," says Krengel, "which, in turn, makes a kitchen feel roomier."

If you suspect you've got some expendable areas such as these but aren't sure how to incorporate them, call in a certified kitchen designer, remodeling contractor, interior designer, or spatial planner. Or talk to a design consultant at your local home center.

Step 3 BUMP IT OUT

Some of the changes mentioned above are simple, some a bit more complex, but all are relatively economical, provided you do not run into unexpected problems with electrical, plumbing, or heating systems. Somewhat more expensive—because it entails removing part of an exterior wall—a bump-out can add light and precious space to your kitchen.

A bump-out is a cantilevered addition that extends interior space but doesn't require a new foundation or modifications to an existing foundation—the room simply gets "bumped out" to hang a few feet off the house. The smallest versions in this category are the

mini-greenhouse windows and bump-out bays that can be installed over an existing window opening. Often used in kitchens, these little additions can brighten things up a bit, but they don't add any floor space.

With a bump-out addition however, you will gain some square footage—not much, but enough to make a difference in a cramped kitchen. Bump-outs often feature windows on three sides, which usher light into the whole room and make a pleasant eating area; this in turn releases space in the kitchen for more storage or a larger food-prep zone. A bump-out with fewer windows and more wall space could accommodate storage cabinets and work counters.

OPPOSITE

To make way for a small eat-in area and pantry, the homeowners closed off a closet in an adjacent room and made it accessible from the kitchen with sliding glass doors. Eliminating cabinets under the window made room for the petite table and chairs.

ABOVE

Because they flow into adjoining areas, open-plan kitchens provide a fluid sense of space. But it is important to establish boundaries that prevent household traffic from straying into the path of a busy cook. Here, half-walls and an island clearly define the work area and conceal the cooking and cleanup mess.

RIGHT

Color and light can transform the way a cramped kitchen looks, but new appliances can make a tiny space more efficient, especially when you can't add on. Here, light-colored cabinets, excellent task lighting, and new stainless-steel appliances vastly improve a space-challenged floor plan.

making the best of it

There are a couple of ways, as you can see, to open up your kitchen a little bit and make it work better for you. But in many cases—unless you decide to invest in a major remodel—it will still be a small kitchen. Let go of the fantasy that the room can be multifunctional—you may have space enough to do some paperwork or menu planning or help your kids with a crafts project or have a cup of coffee with a friend or prepare a fabulous meal with another cook, but you probably can't do all of these things at the same time.

Learn to love and accept your kitchen for what it is—a meal-preparation and cleanup center. Even if it's not possible to expand its dimensions, you can work with what you've got to make the room function well and feel comfortable.

First, take a look at the layout. Is it an efficient work space?

Do you like cooking with another person, and if so, does your current layout make that possible? What is the most serious flaw in your kitchen. Not enough floor space? Insufficient counter space? A claustrophobic feeling? Too much household traffic in and out of the work zone? A little tweaking may be all you need to make the layout work better for you.

Adding an island can solve many layout problems, defining the work zone and directing traffic away from it, providing more counter space, and supplying supplemental storage. An island can also function as a mini-eating area, replacing a table and chairs that may be crowding the room.

No space for an island? You may be able to fit a peninsula counter in somewhere; it, too, will give you more storage and work space.

You may also be able to solve layout problems by simply moving the refrigerator, repositioning the sink, or investing in small-scale appliances that are geared for compact kitchens such as yours. (See "Scale Down Your Appliances," below.)

Many books and magazines articles have been written about the work triangle, kitchen layouts, suggested clearances, and so forth. Take advantage of these resources to figure out what your problem is—you may come across an easy solution. If not, seek professional help. You can turn the entire job over to someone or pay for just a consultation to get you on the right track. Says Lori Krengel, "Kitchens by Krengel is a full-service firm—from idea to finished kitchen—but occasionally we do consultations. For an hourly rate we'll spend an hour or two talking about the project with the homeowners, then offer some ideas. If the clients want drawings and specifications, too, it generally costs from several hundred to a thousand dollars. But it's money well spent because the drawings can go right to a remodeling contractor and speed the job along."

scale down your appliances

The huge side-by-side refrigerator-freezer is no longer the norm, especially in a space-conscious kitchen. Nowadays you can chose small under-counter models with a 6.1-cubic-foot capacity, space-saving drawer-style units that can be placed wherever it's most convenient, or even tall and narrow "columns" for keeping food cold or freezing it. At least one majjor manufacturer offers a "fresh-food" column, which ranges from 24 to 30 inches wide; a freezer column, available as narrow as 18 inches wide; and a skinny wine cooler with a beverage compartment that measures only 18 inches wide yet cools five bottles of wine and sixty 12-ounce cans of other beverages.

For cooking, there are scaled-down ranges as narrow as 20 inches; compact microwave ovens (one microwave in a drawer mounts just under a countertop); and drawer-size dishwashers. One of kitchen designer Lori Krengel's favorites space-saving choices is a convection microwave, which she says, can stand in for a conventional oven for most needs.

You can now reduce counter clutter with small appliances that do double-duty—a toaster-toaster-oven combination, for example; a food processor that is also a blender; or a "drink station" that is reputed to brew more than 30 kinds of hot drinks, in single servings, including coffee, tea, hot chocolate, and cappuccino.

OPPOSITE
Thanks to a well-designed layout and a harmonious color scheme, this small kitchen is highly efficient. The compact multifunctional island supplies storage, work space, and a mini-eating area.

Update Storage

Perhaps insufficient—or possibly *inefficient*—storage is the big problem in your kitchen. If your cabinets are jammed so full that things spill out onto counters and other surfaces, no wonder you're feeling squeezed.

The first step to improving storage is to purge all parts of the room of unnecessary items. With kitchen space at a premium, clutter definitely has to go.

Look through all of the drawers and cabinets; check the counters. Do you ever use that juicer that was such a good idea two Christmases ago? How about the crock pot? Do you really need 20 wooden spoons for stirring? Once you get rid of useless items that are clogging the cupboards and covering the counters your kitchen will immediately feel larger—and it will function more efficiently, too.

The next step—find a way to store the items that remain. We're not suggesting that you buy new cabinets, but you may want to retrofit your existing ones with handy inserts that store more. Some of these storage aids include segmented or tiered drawer inserts for flatware and cutlery; vertical dividers for trays, baking sheets, and cutting boards; wire racks for the insides of cabinet doors; lazy Susans for blind-corner cabinets or pantry cabinets; spice-drawer inserts; pullout bins for trash or recycling; and much more. Check local home centers, cabinet showrooms, or on-line sites for items that may be useful for you.

If you plan to replace your cabinets, consider the three-drawer base units that many kitchen specialists prefer to the standard one-drawer, one-cupboard models. In the newer units, the top drawer is the normal size, but the bottom two are extra deep and very handy for organizing pots and pans, casserole dishes, mixing bowls, even everyday china. And they pull all the way out so that you can see the entire contents without kneeling down and poking around.

Islands and tall pantry cabinets are storage workhorses. If there's space, add one—or both—of these to your kitchen to contain clutter and improve organization. And you don't have to reserve the pantry for canned and packaged foods; you can also use it for pots and pans, dishes, even small appliances.

Some built-in kitchen islands are chock full of storage capacity, with cupboards, shelves, nooks, and crannies all around, not to mention work space on the top. But if your kitchen's physical dimensions don't permit access to all sides of the island, don't bother to invest in one. Instead, think about bringing in a ready-made small-scale model, a slim table built to countertop height, or an island on wheels that can roll out of the way if needed. (The latter is a good idea only if you have a convenient place for it.) These alternatives come in many sizes and styles, and some offer a good amount of storage as well as an extra food-prep surface.

Point-of-use storage save steps and time, so organize your kitchen to place cookware near the range, dishes and glasses close to the sink, and dishwasher in cabinets or on shelves that are easy to reach. Stow items that you don't use every day in higher and lower cabinets. Unless you've got plenty of space left in the cabinets, find a spot outside of the kitchen for items you still, but only occasionally, need.

According to many kitchen specialists, extending cabinets all the way to the ceiling can add almost 50 percent to the storage capacity of your kitchen. These high-up units are handy for items you don't often use, and the vertical sweep of cabinetry creates the illusion of greater height and makes the room look more streamlined.

Countertop clutter in a small kitchen shrinks the work space considerably. Counters typically measure 24 inches deep, and because the first 18 inches are literally within an arm's reach, they get most of the active use. You can begin the battle on

OPPOSITE LEFT

Stretching the cabinets all the way to the ceiling increases the perception of vertical space while providing additional storage for items seldom used but still needed. Another space expander at work in this kitchen is the depth of the appliances, which matches that of the cabinets for a smooth, slimming line.

OPPOSITE RIGHT

Small but sunny, this kitchen boasts well-organized storage. Glass-front cabinets near the main sink hold dinnerware and glasses; bowls and baking dishes are stored in the island. Tall cupboards near the door serve as a pantry for dry goods.

TOP RIGHT

Wall cabinets would have felt oppressive in this older but still charming tiny kitchen. A single shelf positioned a few feet from the ceiling leads the eye up to the openness of the skylight. Open shelves under the counter also lighten the look, putting colorful dishes on display and easy to find.

dish up storage

For everyday dishes, here are several appealing approaches to storage:

■ Store them in large, deep drawers. Line the bottom of the drawers with pegboard, and use movable pegs to corral plates and bowls in neat stacks.
■ Plate racks, on their own or integrated into a bank of cabinetry, put your dishware on display while keeping it handy.
■ If you intend to use a built-in plate rack for drying your dishes, make sure it's installed where the wet dishes can drip into the sink, either directly or by means of a drainboard.
■ Should you choose to keep dishes in a cupboard, check out the array of minishelves that allow you to separately stack plates of different diameters so that you can easily get access to them one at a time.
■ A word about glass-fronted cabinets: unless you have immaculately kept cupboards, artfully filled with beautiful glassware and dishes, think twice before giving the all-clear on this door-style option. Instead, consider using seeded, ribbed, frosted, or tinted glass panels on the doors. You'll still reap the benefits from a lighter look, but you won't have to suffer the full exposure of your cabinets' not-too-neat or attractive contents.

clutter by keeping this frontage clear and using the 6 inches nearest the wall or backsplash for frequently used items such as a coffeemaker, toaster, or canisters. Or invest in one or two appliance garages to neatly contain the small electrics you use routinely.

Counters often get cluttered with messages, mail, appointment cards, and so forth. Move this mess by hanging a shelf or two on the wall away from the work zone and designating it the message center. Or as Lori Krengel suggests, hang a dry-erase board on the side of the refrigerator or a tall cabinet. "It keeps the counters clear and makes a very efficient message center," she says, "and tucked away on the side of the fridge, it maintains a clean visual line."

Contrary to popular wisdom, hanging often-used items on the wall or from ceiling racks is not a smart strategy—it may provide accessible storage, but it also creates visual clutter. "I find pot racks distracting, and somewhat unsanitary, with all that grease and dust flying around," says interior designer Patricia Gaylor of Little Falls, New Jersey. Lori Krengel agrees. "I generally advise clients to get rid of all their junky pots and pans, choose three or four that are important, and put them in a cabinet or deep storage drawer. Pots and pans on display seldom add to the aesthetics of a kitchen."

smart tip

EASY ACCESS

The plastic or vinyl shoe organizers that are typically found in bedroom closets can do wonders in the kitchen. Hang one or two on the inside of pantry-cabinet door, and use them for the small items that get lost on shelves— packets of tea, granola bars, jars of seldom-used spices.

Expand Visually

Once you have updated the layout, decluttered the counters and cabinets, and devised a good storage system, you'll find that your kitchen has become more functional and comfortable. If it still seems small and a bit confining, it's time to resort to some fool-the-eye tricks that will make it look—and feel—larger.

"In a small space, simple and streamlined is best," says Patricia Gaylor. No, you don't have to create an austere design that reveals nothing of your tastes and personality—just reduce visual clutter to a minimum.

Keeping cabinets, walls, and floors the same color—or at least in the same color family—simplifies the look of the room and lets the eye roam freely. Although all-white, neutral, or pastel kitchens look especially bright and airy, color is not as important as unity. Cabinets in light wood tones can also look light and expansive, especially if they are paired with floors and counters in a similar shade. Keep the cabinets themselves simple, choosing clean-lined door styles rather than elaborate Old World designs, and if possible, align them with the appliances for continuous, unbroken plane.

You can brighten a dark and dismal kitchen quickly and economically by painting the walls and painting or staining the existing cabinets. Talk to your local paint dealer about the best way to prepare cabinets for refurbishing. And once the work is done, replace fussy or elaborate hardware with sleek and simple pulls and knobs.

Another way to open up space is to reduce the oppressive feeling that comes from a mass of cabinets at eye level—replace solid doors with glass ones, or remove the cabinet doors entirely, painting the insides a light color that harmonizes with the rest of the room.

If keeping cabinet contents neat is not your idea of a fun activity, opt for frosted or sand-blasted glass instead of clear doors—or no glass at all.

You can also get rid of upper cabinets completely and use open shelves instead. This is a very effective space-stretching strategy as long as you keep the shelves relatively neat. Fill them with dishes you use every day intermingled with a few favorite pieces, or devote them solely to a display of collectibles. If you follow the design principles of balance and symmetry, the shelves will add pizzazz while they open up visual space.

Some other tips that may work in your kitchen—choose shiny surfaces and diagonal patterns for floors, countertops, and backsplashes; eliminate clutter on counters, islands, and the front of the refrigerator; and trim appliances with panels that match the cabinets.

Lighting, windows, and even a bit of mirror here and there are essential for creating an airy open ambiance, and they are discussed in depth in Chapter 6.

smart tip

STORAGE STAND-INS

Kitchen cabinets and counters filled to the brim? Think about storing some items in other rooms. For example, give cookbooks their own section on the living-room bookshelves. Find space for the good china in the dining room. If you only use it once or twice a year, stow it in the basement, attic, or garage—or sell it on e-Bay. Display your best-looking serving dishes on the dining-room sideboard, on the wall, or on a living room tabletop filled with small objects that you love to look at.

OPPOSITE
Even minimal amounts of countertop clutter can make a space-challenged kitchen inefficient and messy. This narrow cupboard helps solve that problem by containing spice jars and other small items, then smoothly pulling out to make them easily accessible.

BELOW
If you are relatively neat, consider replacing bulky wall cabinets with open shelves, especially if you have dishes and glasses you wouldn't mind putting on display.

design workbook
SPACE-STRETCHING STRATEGIES

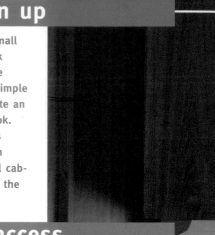

lighten up

In an ultra-small U-shape work area, a subtle palette and simple cabinets create an expansive look. Open shelves alternate with standard wall cabinets to keep the mood light.

easy access

A glass-fronted cabinet, top left, stores dishes and glasses close to the sink and dishwasher.

organization solutions

Clever storage minimizes clutter. (See also far left.) A cutting board slides out as needed; file-style pullouts hold cookbooks; and drawers keep assorted utensils handy.

cornering clutter

Corner space becomes useful, middle left.

recycling center

Behind a cabinet door lies a spot for recyclables. (See also left.) The work counter lifts up for access.

design workbook
AN ATTRACTIVE, EFFICIENT GALLEY

understated beauty

A neutral color scheme, sleek cabinets with simple pulls, and a minimum of counter clutter maximize linear and square footage space in this small galley kitchen.

slick materials

Small glass tiles on the back-splash reflect light beautifully. (See also top left.) Freestanding metal sheets are used to hang utensils and a compact pot filler faucet saves trips to the sink.

a smooth line

The built-in wall ovens and refrigerator, far left, are flush with the counters, saving floor space and maintaining the sleek kitchen design.

sink sculpture

A compact pull-out spray faucet, left, is both practical and good-looking—perfect for a streamlined kitchen.

design workbook

A KITCHEN IN A LOFT

this wall works

The refrigerator, ovens, and dry storage are compactly located in a freestanding wall that divides the loft space.

unencumbered area

The configuration of cabinets and counters leaves plenty of room in the food-preparation and cleanup zones.

unobstructed view

Natural light streams in easily because there are no upper cabinets over the counter with the sinks, top left.

fresh idea

A vented exhaust system, left, prevents odors from permeating the open loft's living and sleeping areas.

clean surfaces

Under-mounted sinks and a solid-surface countertop look clean—and there's no rim to collect crumbs.

design workbook
MAXIMIZING EXISTING SPACE

good cabinet choice

New cabinetry makes better use of the space in this long, narrow kitchen. (See the "before" photo, bottom far left.)

expansive ideas

Sticking with white cabinets and refraining from covering up the windows keeps the space bright.

smart and stylish

Mirrored doors not only look elegant but make the room appear larger—plus they hide what's inside.

optimal illumination

Recessed fixtures provide good ambient light; under-cabinet spotlights brighten the work surfaces, top left.

neat idea

A built-in cupboard, left, is an attractive solution to countertop clutter and a handsome display space.

 baths

In many American houses, both old and new, a large bathroom is a rare occurrence. Before you embark on a campaign to make yours larger, keep in mind that in the bath—as well as in any room of your house—bigger does not always translate to better. A 1,000-square-foot floor plan may impress the neighbors and wind up featured in a design magazine, but chances are that it doesn't function any better than one with 100 square feet.

Structural and financial concerns may force you to give up your fantasies of an enormous jetted tub, separate shower, long grooming counters, or a spa-like sauna. Even so, you don't have to be content with cramped conditions. This chapter will guide you toward a dreamy bath with suggestions for making the most of the space you have.

LEFT
This neutral color scheme makes a small bath look appreciably larger. A strip of decorative wall tile adds design interest.

bath basics

Bathrooms are like kitchens in one important way—the activities that take place must be supported by appliances, fixtures, fittings, electricity, and plumbing. It's necessary to have sufficient space in the bath for all of these activities, equipment, and systems, but it isn't required—or even particularly desirable—to have palatial surroundings. Huge bathrooms often look cold and austere, can be difficult and expensive to heat, and are not necessarily more useful than small ones.

A tiny cramped bathroom is no picnic either, of course. And until recently, that's exactly the type of bath most houses and apartments offered. If you're dealing with one of these space-challenged baths, there are many things—some structural, some cosmetic—you can do to improve it.

How much space do you really need in a bath? As long as there is ample room for the fixtures, a place to keep linens and grooming items, and a visual ambiance that encourages relaxation, it's probably fine.

smart steps
make it live larger

Step 1   SEEK OUT EXTRA SPACE

Short of building an addition, what can you do to expand your bathroom? Apply the same premise to bath expansion that you've used in other rooms in the house—consider knocking down a wall or borrowing space from an adjoining area.

If you own one of the millions of older houses that populate the cities, towns, and rural areas of this country, you've probably got great expansion potential. Some of these houses boast four and five bedrooms or several bedrooms and a sewing room, spaces that many of today's families don't need. As flush as they were with bedrooms, theses houses often had only one bath; once in a while an extra bath was appended to the master bedroom, but it was usually tiny, more like an afterthought.

In these cases, annexing a linen closet or bedroom closet or taking space from an extra bedroom to significantly increase the size of a bath are typical ways to

OPPOSITE
Tiling up to the ceiling and elevating the tub on a platform creates the impression of a grander space.

BELOW
An under-mounted lav offers a bit more space on a countertop or the sink's deck area.

RIGHT
Think creatively when seeking storage for the bath. A case in point: in typically wasted space above the toilet, two shelves hold neatly rolled towels.

expand, says interior designer Tracey Stephens of Montclair, New Jersey. "You have to rearrange a couple of doorways, but that's not a big problem because you're redoing the rest of the space anyway."

Auxiliary areas that can be annexed for bathroom space also abound in these older houses—odd little hallways, a couple of seldom-used hall closets, or bedroom closets that back up to existing bathrooms. Sometimes these areas are just large enough to enclose a shower or to supply an alcove for a tub. Breaking through the back of a bedroom closet and outfitting it with shelves can garner valuable storage for towels, toilet paper, extra soaps, and so forth. None of these alterations adds much in terms of square footage, perhaps, but they can free up enough floor space to make the bath function better and feel bigger.

Does your bath have a bulky radiator? "Take it out and install radiant heating (under the floor) instead," says Stephens. "It's much nicer, and you'll gain some wall space."

Step 2   ADD A BAY OR BUMP-OUT

Adding dormers, expansive bays, or little cantilevered bump-out additions can enlarge small baths enough to make a big difference. Even if the space in question is on the second story of your house, these projects are still doable.

A bay or other type of bump-out can become a sunny alcove for a tub; a dormer could contain a toilet, a storage cabinet, or a little window seat with storage underneath. And all of these alterations will make the existing dimensions of the room seem larger.

Because these "additions" are small, they do not require the support of a foundation. But if you plan to furnish them with a bathtub or other heavy object, consult an architect, engineer, or your local building authority to make sure the structure can carry the additional load.

Step 3   UPDATE THE LAYOUT

If there's no way to expand the dimensions of your bath, consider modifying the layout. You may be surprised to discover that a few minor changes in the floor plan can appreciably enhance usability and comfort.

Perhaps there's not enough space between the lav and toilet, or maybe the room would work better with the toilet placed on another wall. And while you're assessing the layout, consider giving up the tub or tub-with-shower unit in favor of a roomy separate shower. Tubs take up a lot of space; if you don't routinely use one, why not splurge on a fancy spa shower?

Even if you come up with what seems to be a better layout, keep in mind that moving fixtures is not a job for a novice. You'll need a plumber—and you'll need to be conversant with minimum clearances required by local codes. See "Accessible Fixture Placement," on page 72, for widely accepted clearances, and check them against the changes you're planning.

BELOW

Because of their clean lines, emphasis on glass and other natural materials, and minimalist approach to decoration, contemporary-style bathrooms are a step ahead of other styles in making small dimensions look larger.

RIGHT

Adding a bathroom to an attic space can pose problems. Here, the homeowners raised the ceiling to the rafters and added a roof window, making this tight corner more comfortable and appealing.

BELOW RIGHT

Making good use of another small space, the owners installed a roomy vanity cabinet in an alcove.

Using Small-Scale Fixtures

If it's not possible to expand or even change the layout of the room, think about investing in smaller-size bath fixtures. In a cramped space, using a smaller-than-average toilet, lav, or tub can have a huge impact.

When shopping for pint-sized fixtures you'll find that showrooms carry the widest and most expensive selection of items and custom options, but you can place a special order. Check out large home centers and plumbing-supply outlets, too, and browse the Internet for an overall picture of what's available.

There are many small-scale lavs from which to choose—wall mounted, corner, and pedestal styles. All of them are great space-savers. But before you buy, do a dry run—can you get your hands in the basin and under the faucet for washing? Small sinks are generally fitted with standard-size faucets; to maximize space in the basin, position the fittings in the corner of the lav or choose single-control or wall-mounted fittings.

LEFT
Pedestal lavs consume less floor space than standard vanities but don't offer storage. In this bath, a generously proportioned medicine cabinet compensates for that loss.

OPPOSITE
A vessel-style (above-counter) lav is not only fashionable, but practical in a bathroom that is storage challenged, freeing the space normally taken inside the cabinet by a drop-in basin.

smart tip ACCESSIBLE FIXTURE PLACEMENT

The table below shows the minimum floor clearances, in inches, recommended by the National Kitchen and Bath Association (NKBA) for placing fixtures in a bathroom that meets accessible design criteria. If you don't have enough floor space to meet them, at least use these minimum clearances as guidelines, but tailor them to your personal situation and available space as necessary.

FIXTURE	NKBA MINIMUM
Lavatory	30 x 48*
Toilet	48 x 48**
Bidet	48 x 48***
Bathtub	60 x 30****

In the case of a shower that is less than 60 inches wide, the minimum clearance should be 36 inches deep by the width of the shower plus 12 inches. A shower that is more than 60 inches wide requires 36 inches of clear floor space by the width of the shower.

* Up to 19 inches can extend under the lavatory.
** At least 16 inches must extend to each centerline of the toilet.
*** You may reduce it to 30 x 48 if space is tight, but that may compromise full use.
**** For a parallel approach. For a perpendicular approach, clearance should be 60 x 48.

If you choose a wall-hung or pedestal sink, you'll save floor space and achieve a lighter look but loose storage. If that will be a problem for you, rethink the vanity—they're not all space hogs; in fact, some new versions measure as little as 13 inches deep and 18 inches wide, compared with standard varieties that run about 18 inches deep and 24 inches wide. Look for one that offers custom features such as organizational aids and handy toe-kick storage.

Toilets are available in a wide array of size and shapes—round bowl, elongated bowl, compact elongated bowl, one piece, two piece, and wall hung. One-piece toilets, with their low tanks, look smaller but are actually the same size as two-piece models. At the moment, a one-piece toilet that measures about 25 inches front to back is the smallest that the industry offers.

The mega-bath for which so many people yearn is dominated by a huge whirlpool tub, often set on a regal platform. You may have to forget that fantasy, but you can still take a soothing bath in a small bathroom. Extra-deep soaking tubs come in standard sizes, as do whirlpools, which are now are available with either water or air jets. Corner tubs, made specifically for tight quarters, are widely available. Some of the newer alcove-style tubs measure a mere 4 feet long. Or a 29 x 36-inch tub-shower unit that includes built-in soap dishes, shelves, and a seat might be the answer to your space problems.

Instead of a tub—or in addition to one—how about an angled shower, which will fit neatly into a corner? Here's where one of those annexed closets may be helpful, providing a place for the separate shower you couldn't fit in originally.

smart tip PLANNING

The easiest and least costly remodels take advantage of the existing water supplies, drain lines, and vent stacks. If you want to add a bath or expand one, try locating it next to an existing one. Even stacking the rooms one over the other on different floors can take advantage of the existing lines and lower the cost of building or rebuilding the bath. Another cost-cutting measure is limiting the plumbing fixtures to two walls. This avoids the need for—and expense of—additional plumbing lines.

addressing the mess

If you have been able to beg, borrow, or steal some extra square footage, you gained actual space for your bath. But don't stop there. By using some design savvy, you can also gain apparent space, making the room look—and feel—larger than it really is.

But first, remember that clutter is space enemy number one; and because your bath has probably been short on storage as well as space, clutter may have collected, making the room

A chest of drawers, little shelves, and a collection of clever cubbyholes provide varied and plentiful storage in this bathroom, keeping the other surfaces neat and clutter free. The large mirror reflects the other half of the room, a tried-and-true method for expanding visual space.

feel even smaller. Do a purge, getting rid of expired medicines, old cosmetics, frayed and torn towels, and anything else you don't need. Then look around for potential storage.

Typically underutilized, the wall above the toilet is a good spot for a shallow cabinet or a set of open shelves. Other areas for handy shelves include the space above a doorway, inside the shower, at the end of the tub, or any place there is a free wall. Seek space for attractive hooks and wooden pegs, too, on the back of the door, between the toilet and sink, and next to the tub. If you plan to hang damp towels on any of these hooks, be sure air will circulate freely around them.

Make the vanity cupboard work harder by outfitting it with storage aids like the ones you'll be using in the kitchen. If the vanity has a drawer, use an insert to organize it. Any sink that doesn't allow for a vanity cabinet—pedestal or wall hung, for example—can be skirted with pretty fabric that hides cleaning supplies or other essentials. Assess your medicine cabinet—perhaps you have room for a larger one, with a larger mirror, which will increase the sense of space and magnify available light. Some models offer deep storage that can hold rolls of tissue or blow dryers. A sleek, frameless cabinet will also stretch space.

"People are always looking for more storage in the bath," says Tracey Stephens. "One way to get it is to cut out a portion of wallboard and install shallow cabinets or shelving between the studs." These nifty niches can hold medicines, toiletries, or rolled-up towels. A long between-the-studs cabinet can combine shelves on top with a small laundry hamper on the bottom; a few niches near the toilet can contain extra rolls of tissue.

With space at a premium, you may have to look for storage outside the bath. Extra towels, toilet paper, soaps, and shampoos can be stowed in a linen closet, a handsome cabinet, or a chest of drawers in the hall just outside.

Creating effective storage that banishes clutter and restores order is an important part of expanding your bath visually. The next step is to simplify the look of the room to help open up space and make it appear less crowded.

There are no rules for stretching bath space visually, but there are plenty of opinions. Some design experts recommend painting the walls a light color. White can seem a bit sterile in a bath, but creamy off-whites, pale beiges, and pastels offer a little more warmth and create that sought-after visual serenity. Other designers disagree with the pale-color theory, advising the use of deeper, richer tones for a cozy and intimate ambiance. But most agree on the wisdom of sticking with one color or color family. A single floor color—preferably light—and walls that complement both the fixtures and the floor will make the room look bigger, they say.

Most design pros also agree that it's important to avoid fussiness and to aim for a unified look. Use paint instead of wallpaper, for example, unless the paper's design is very simple with a lot of white space; select a clear-glass shower door rather than a patterned curtain; choose floor tile in large sizes and avoid cutesy, decorative details; and paint moldings, baseboards, and doors the same color as the walls. Bath experts also suggest focusing on horizontal line rather than vertical, pointing out that making a very small room seem taller can actually shrink visual space. Keep window treatments to a minimum—good options are mini-blinds, shades, or simple gauzy curtains. If it suits your decorating scheme and privacy concerns, unadorned windows are also a good option. Open shelves enhance visual flow better than solid, dense wall cabinets and keep things conveniently within reach. But if they look busy and messy, that visual flow is lost. Reserve them for neatly rolled or stacked towels and decorative bottles and jars. And paint them the same color as the walls.

Go easy on accessories—they can quickly become clutter. The hooks or wooden pegs that have been suggested to augment storage should sport towels that match each other and complement the color of the walls. A mélange of towel patterns qualifies as clutter.

Mirrors, windows, glass block, and adequate lighting are all key space-stretching strategies as well. These are discussed in depth in Chapter 8, beginning on page 152.

The consensus? Your best bet for visually enlarging a small bath is a light color scheme, a minimum of accessories, no fussy detail, and a simple window treatment. All well and good, but is that a look you could love? If not, you will have to obey the only hard-and-fast decorating rule—please yourself.

Instead of following the dictates of others, look at magazines that cover bathroom design and visit showrooms. It's true that a creamy-white bath will look bright and airy, but vivid color and splashy details may make you happier. And if you create a room that you think is fabulous and interesting, you won't even be aware of its size.

design workbook
BORROWED SPACE SAVES THE DAY

compact convenience

Using square footage from adjoining areas, designer Tracey Stephens transformed a cramped bath into a spalike retreat that now features an air-jetted tub and shower. (See also top left and bottom near left.)

seamless blend

The new bath blends perfectly with the home's original turn-of-the-century architecture, thanks to nostalgic white "subway" tiles and fixtures and fittings with period styling.

space savvy

Shelves fit neatly into a niche that would otherwise go unused, far left. The designer also squeezed in a steam shower, left, by annexing space from a hallway closet. Another clever use of space is the narrow but useful new linen closet located between the shower and the entrance to the bathroom.

before

design workbook
PATTERN ADDS PRESENCE

all dressed up

Rescued from blandness, this miniscule powder room now glows with rich color and lively pattern. Although it breaks the "rule" that discourages large pattern in small rooms, the toile wallcovering actually makes a significant design splash. Other enlivening details include framed prints, classical moldings, and a solid-color wainscot to offset the pattern.

richly detailed

A large mirror magnifies the light in the room, left. Sconces are attached directly to the mirror's frame.

banishing the blahs

The pale color scheme in the original powder room, top left, may have visually expanded space, but because it lacked detail and depth, it made the room look boring. Sometimes, more is more interesting.

design workbook
BATH IN A PRETTY GLASS BOX

space conservation

Tinted sliding glass doors make way for a small master bathroom in this converted industrial space.

oh, what a feeling

Quiet colors, minimalist design, and tiny spotlights add to the room's peaceful ambiance.

shower simplicity

A modest-size glass shower is situated in a corner next to the toilet, top left. Glass enhances the open sense.

points of light

Artful lighting inside and outside the room helps to set the mood for relaxation and pampering.

bathed in beauty

Open doors reveal a soaking tub, left. The deck-mounted faucet's design matches the vessel's simplicity.

design workbook
BEACH COTTAGE BEAUTY

ocean hues

Deep sea-blue walls and pristine white bead board put a fresh face on this beach cottage bathroom. Vintage-style and refurbished older fixtures get a boost from pretty details, such as the new faucets and fittings.

neat nook

The owners built storage, top left, against a wall at the end of the tub for towels, soaps, and toiletries. The open cube design also provides a handsome display.

style revival

This nostalgic console lav is open underneath, so it does expose the plumbing. However, it's got great legs. Also, unlike most pedestal lavs, this style has a spacious deck, where there is adequate space for grooming aids and extra soap. (See also left.)

5

furnishings

FUNCTION, STYLE, AND COST   USING FURNITURE EFFECTIVELY
DESIGN WORKBOOK

Frustrated and intimidated by the physical parameters of less-than-generous spaces, many people are tempted to cram in every bit of furniture they can, no matter what size. You know the importance of scale and proportion, but do you still give in to the temptation to over-furnish? Then you could be making your home feel and look smaller and more restrictive. Small spaces are not always inherently flawed. You could be mistaken if you believe that a modest amount of space is incapable of functioning effectively unless you max out every square inch with furnishings. Any space that is cluttered will be chaotic and dysfunctional. Instead, learn to furnish pint-sized spaces to make them every bit as efficient, good-looking, and comfortable as larger ones. The trick, say design experts, is to proceed carefully and logically.

function, style, and cost

To suitably furnish any room, but especially one that is small, you'll need to first consider the function of both the furniture and the space itself. Can the furniture be versatile so that it can satisfy multipurpose needs? Will the pieces get daily wear and tear or only occasional use? Will they be casual or formal, built-in, modular, or movable?

Once you've answered those questions, it's fine to think of style—traditional, country, contemporary, or perhaps a mix. To avoid shopping anxiety, narrow your choices by taking cues from your decorative preferences, the other elements you've chosen for your scheme, and the overall architectural character of your house. In a formal center-hall Colonial or stately period Victorian you probably won't want ultra-sleek modern pieces, which may look out of place. On the other hand, spare, streamlined pieces would look at home in a contemporary house or a modern loft or apartment. (See "What's Your Style?," on the opposite page.)

Finally, think about cost. Most furniture styles are available in a wide range of prices, from low to high end, with many versions in between. Don't assume that paying top dollar means you're buying the best—only durable materials and solid construction can guarantee that. But if an item is very cheap, beware—there has probably been skimping done somewhere, either in the manufacturing process or in the finishing work.

To all of these considerations add the issue of size—the physical limitations of the room will have a significant impact on the furniture that you choose. (See "Why Size Counts," on page 78.)

Furniture Placement

Design professionals often recommend specific clearances to follow when arranging furniture. These are not strict rules, especially in small rooms, but you might find them useful as starting points or as tools for making your small spaces more functional. You can always rework these recommended clearances to suit your own tastes, the lifestyle of your household, and the size of the room, keeping in mind that the only "rule" is to make the space comfortable for the people who are using it.

what's your style?

Thinking in terms of the three major furniture styles will help you choose the pieces that express your tastes and enhance the function of your small spaces. Remember that within each category there are several styles that work together nicely.

Traditional pieces take their cue from designs that were created before 1900 and are often said to have a timeless look. The original designs were often named for influential people—Queen Anne chairs, Chippendale tables, for example—or for specific architectural styles—Baroque, Gothic, Victorian. The emphasis is on rich dark woods, decorative details, curvy, graceful shapes, and highly textured upholstery, often with elaborate trim.

The hallmark of *modern* furniture, the name given to styles created post World War I, is simplicity, spareness, and lack of ornamentation. ("Contemporary" is often interchanged with "modern," although, strictly speaking, it means "of the moment.") The emphasis is on clean geometric lines and natural materials, including wood, metal, stone, glass, leather, even plastic. Because modern styles are generally unfettered by extraneous ornamentation, they are especially good choices for small spaces, as long as upholstered pieces are not oversized.

Country furniture is casual and relaxed. It often has a period feel but, unlike genteel traditional pieces, its sensibility inclines toward the rustic. Tables, chairs, and storage pieces are usually made of pine or oak and are often painted rather than stained. Tailored upholstered pieces in solids and simple prints work well in small rooms.

OPPOSITE
An open plan lives large, allowing plenty of space between pieces of furniture and an unobstructed aisle for traffic.

TOP RIGHT
The glass-top metal table and clean-lined chairs are ideal choices for a small contemporary space.

BOTTOM RIGHT
An elegant wood end table keeps a low profile in a traditional-style interior. With two drawers, it is a compact storage piece.

smart steps
all around the house

Step 1 ANALYZE THE LIVING ROOM

In some houses, the living room is slightly formal, the place where we entertain and put our best foot forward. In other households, it's the place, along with the family room, where we relax in front of the TV, listen to music, read, or just hang. Whether it's used every day or only on special occasions, your living room should offer an attractive, comfortable arrangement of furniture.

If you entertain in the living room, you'll want clearances that your guests can easily navigate. Professionals recommend that you allow 4 to 10 feet between the couch and chairs. In a small room, you will not have the luxury of placing these pieces 10 feet apart; but to avoid crowding, try to follow the 4-foot rule as closely as possible. To permit comfortable legroom, position the coffee table no less than 14 and no more than 18 inches from the couch.

If you watch TV in the living room or family room, take another hint from the pros, who suggest that for optimal viewing the distance between the screen and the seating located opposite it should be three times the size of the screen. Thus, if you've got a 30-inch TV screen, you should sit 90 inches away from it.

Should your space-challenged living room be large enough to do double duty as a home office or dining area, be sure to organize it so that the functions do not interfere with each other. Ideally, you should have a traffic lane that is at least 3 feet wide so that you can move smoothly from one zone to another. If you don't have that kind of floor space, look for storage pieces in which you can stow your office supplies when you're not working or choose a dining table with drop leaves that fold down when the table's not in use.

Step 2 SIZE UP EATING AREAS

The table, of course, is the centerpiece of any eating area, whether it's located in the dining room, in a section of the living room, or in a corner of the kitchen. And seating around that table should be comfortable.

Good space planning calls for enough room to get

LEFT
Instead of a bulky L-shaped piece, a modest loveseat and a medium-size sofa offer comfortable seating and space for an end table in this living room. To allow for a large country-style coffee table, where snacks are served and games are played, the homeowners had to forgo recommended clearances. The arrangement is cozy and suits the family's relaxed lifestyle. Built-in units flanking the fireplace provide space for a TV and storage.

up, down, and around easily. A seated adult takes up a space that is about 20 inches deep but needs 12 to 16 inches more to push back the chair and stand. Placing chairs at angles to the wall can save a few inches but you'll need a round or square table to achieve that.

Rectangular tables require 24 inches per person and 32 to 36 inches of clearance between the table and the wall. On the serving side, table-to-wall distance should be at least 44 inches. If you have the wall area for it, banquette seating saves a significant amount of space.

■ Step 3 ARRANGE THE BEDROOM

Whatever the nature of the bedroom—master suite, kids' room, guest room—it is a place where people sleep; so placement of the bed is the logical first step.

There are clearances to consider here, too. When two people share the room, there should be aisles next to the bed or beds that are wide enough to allow either person to get in and out of bed without walking into a door, bumping into a piece of furniture, or having to climb over the other person.

Establish these clearances by measuring the space on either side of the bed, aiming for 24 inches between the bed and the wall and 36 inches from the bed and any door that opens into the room. If you place two beds side by side, maintain a distance of 18 inches between them. This will allow for a night table and a comfortable aisle for walking.

BELOW
Sunny walls, white furniture and bed linens, and lots of natural light visually expand a tiny attic bedroom. The width of the double bed is 6 inches less than that of a queen-size unit.

OPPOSITE
Restraint is the key in this bedroom. Recessed bookshelves with storage underneath and a shallow desk consume very little floor space, while the gray-painted walls create a calming ambiance.

selecting a sleeper sofa

There's little difference among the pull-out mechanisms in today's sleepers—in fact, most are made by the same company. There's still a support bar under the mattress, but nowadays it curves away from the sleeper's back, allowing a more comfortable sleep. The size and type of mattress are the important variables. The four standard widths include chair size (51–58 in. wide); twin (56–65 in.); double (68–92 in.); and queen (79–101 in.). When you go shopping, take room measurements with you. Make sure there is enough floor space to accommodate the bed when it is unfolded.

Check the mattresses carefully. Because they fold, they won't be as firm as standard models, but many of today's sleeper mattresses are very comfortable. Choices range from innersprings—the more coils the better; 600 and above guaranteeing a good night's sleep—to memory-foam and air-coil mattresses. The latter two provide even more comfort, especially the air coil, which combines an innerspring with an air mattress.

Finally, be bold in the showroom. Sit on the sofa for a few minutes; open and close it once or twice; then lie on it in a couple of positions. There's no other way to gauge its comfort.

using furniture effectively

Before you make final decisions about furnishing a room, identify its existing focal point—or create one. In a field with few hard-and-fast rules, this is rule number one. Focal points, the first thing you notice when you enter a space, are sometimes suggested by a distinctive architectural feature, such as a fireplace, an eye-catching built-in cabinet, or a spectacular window. If your room lacks features such as these, you can create a focal point with furnishings. A strategically placed seating area, a handsome piece of furniture, a beautiful painting, or a dramatic treatment for an otherwise undistinguished window—all of these could qualify. In dining rooms, the focal point is usually the table, although a sideboard or great-looking mirror may be the dominant feature. The latter takes up no floor space, and the glass will reflect light and make even a tiny room appear twice its size. Beautiful linens can draw attention to a bed rather than a large headboard. Another possibility is a canopy that can be suspended from the ceiling.

Once you have established the focal point in your small space, designers advise, arrange the furniture, accessories, and even colors to relate to it and draw the eye toward it. Arranging the room in this way will give it a cohesive center of gravity, pull it together, and make it inviting and comfortable. In a large room two focal points can co-exist as long as they are balanced, but in a small room it's best to settle for one. When too many objects are competing for center stage, the design becomes chaotic and people feel restless. Think back—do you remember being in rooms that made you feel uncomfortable and vaguely uneasy? Chances are that these spaces lacked a focal point and as a result exuded a kind of design chaos that translated itself to you.

Why Size Counts

Design experts differ about the size of furniture that should be used in small rooms. Some say choose small-scale pieces; others say reduce visual clutter and enhance harmony by using larger—and fewer—pieces.

But all agree on keeping it simple. Clean-lined furniture and simple shapes, they say, will create a feeling of calm and

openness. Conversely, pieces with huge curving arms or lots of fussy detail may confuse the eye, as will an overuse of small-size furniture and an overload of accessories. And if you do go for one or two large pieces, be sure they are in scale with the other pieces and features in the room.

If your small living room lacks a focal point, a large piece of furniture can anchor it and pull it together. For this purpose you might select a handsome armoire or a roomy couch with an appropriately sized coffee table in front of it. In a room with an inherent focal point, such as a fireplace, scaled-down furniture lets the eye flow and makes the room feel less crowded.

Ann Grasso of AE Grasso Spatial Design Consultants in Providence, Rhode Island, likes big pieces, but she's not crazy about oversize, 42-inch-deep sofas. "They're a sad waste of space anywhere," she says. "The depth and the arms take up too much room. But in a living area, where it's important to provide comfortable furniture, a fairly large sectional can be a good choice. If it's got slim lines and arms—and there are not a lot of

smart tip

DUELING FOCAL POINTS

If your small space has a built-in focal point, such as a fireplace, you don't want another potential focal point, such as a large must-have storage piece, vying for attention. Not to worry. You can make the storage piece practically disappear by painting it the same color as the walls. It will retreat significantly and no longer demand attention.

LEFT
The furniture here is arranged around a brick fireplace painted white to enhance visual space. Traffic from the entry is directed behind the sofa by the door swing. A large mirror over the mantel and a pale color scheme open up the small but charming space.

ABOVE
A glass-top table in front of dramatic gothic-style doors can be set up for a party without blocking the light in a narrow hallway.

clearing the canvas

If you are having trouble creating a pleasing arrangement of furniture in a room, it can help to remove all of the contents and start from scratch. This is a good idea if you have trouble picturing things on paper or if you aren't going to buy a lot of new furniture and just need a fresh start. If at all possible, completely strip down the room, removing everything, including window treatments, rugs, wall art, and other accessories. This way you can observe the true architectural nature of the space without distractions that influence your perceptions. For example, minus the trappings of curtains, you can see that two windows may be slightly different sizes or installed too close to a corner. Other things you may notice might be odd corners, uneven walls, radiators, or heating registers that are conspicuously located, or any other quirky features that are unique to your home.

Don't be in a rush to start filling up the room again. Live with it empty for a few days so that you can really get a sense of the space. Then slowly begin to bring things back inside, starting with the largest objects. You'll know immediately when you've crossed the line with something that doesn't belong. But you have to be willing to pull back and pare down.

other pieces in the room—it can work even in a small space. Simplicity is the key—it's as important as size."

"I like to use the largest furniture that can fit into a small-scale space," says designer Lucianna Samu of Saratoga, New York. "First, it always looks better than a menagerie of little pieces. Second, I hate it when furniture seems to be jumping all over. Whatever you choose," she cautions, "measure carefully before buying, and arrange the room so that the vacuum cleaner fits through it all."

New Jersey interior designer Helene Goodman, IIDA, says the challenge of small rooms leads homeowners to make two mistakes: "Too much furniture or oversized pieces that may technically fit in the space but because of incorrect proportions make it look even smaller. In a couple of showrooms I visited recently, I noticed how huge the upholstered chairs and sofas were" Goodman says. "Suitable for very large rooms, maybe, but way too big for small or even average-sized ones."

To avoid mistakes that may be costly to correct, Goodman advises, create a scale drawing and let a designer review it. "The furniture may seem to fit on a plan, but an expert eye will catch errors right away," she says. "Some time ago, a client proudly presented me with a drawing that showed how many pieces of furniture she had managed to fit into a small living room. After reviewing it I could see that her guests would virtually have to dive over a club chair to reach the sofa."

Arrangement

A pervasive decorating myth states that placing pieces of furniture close to the walls will somehow make a room seem larger. Not true, say the experts. In fact, positioning pieces so that there is plenty of space around them makes the room feel less crowded.

The farther you can see into and through a room, the larger and more open it seems. Arrange furniture in living spaces to free up floor area, and position individual pieces so that they don't block the windows and doors. Why? The view through a door into another room is a particularly effective way to enhance spaciousness.

To maximize space in a bedroom, forgo elaborate head- and foot-boards and keep the bed low to the ground so that it will appear less massive. Some design experts also suggest using no headboard. They suggest hanging a quilt, a pretty piece of tapestry-like fabric, or a collection of framed photographs over the bed instead.

ABOVE

A modern L-shape sofa provides plenty of seating and streamlines the look of a room, which in turn makes the space feel larger. In this city loft, high ceilings magnify the vertical space and white walls reflect natural light. In keeping with the contemporary character of the loft, exposed ductwork becomes a prominent architectural element.

If you must have a king-size bed in a small space, reduce its massive look by "floating" it on a platform, says Ann Grasso. "All you will see is the bed, not what's elevating it. If you keep the rest of the space clutter free," she says, "this strategy makes for a calm and restful atmosphere."

If sleeping quarters are really tight, beef up the headboard with shelves and cubbyholes to hold reading lights, books, and sundries. Although this kind of headboard will push the bed out into the room by several inches, or even as much as a half a foot,

it will save overall floor space by eliminating the need for night tables and other occasional furniture elsewhere in the room. If you prefer a night table, choose one that offers a couple of drawers for storage.

Keep bedroom furniture to a minimum if possible. When you select bureaus for storing clothes, go for tall chests with deep drawers rather than long and low triple dressers. The vertical pieces will lead the eye up and at the same time consume a minimum of wall space.

OPPOSITE
A couple of fool-the-eye strategies make this small bedroom look spacious and serene: keeping it simple and using the wall as a stand-in for a headboard, selecting airy little bedside tables, and eliminating clutter.

RIGHT
A cozy bedroom is tucked under the eaves, with salvaged barn beams providing rustic design interest. Built-ins recessed all the way into the walls hold clothes, books, and other paraphernalia, leaving floor space free for the bed.

BELOW
A comfortable daybed can instantly convert this home office into a guest room. Clean-lined furniture and a cohesive color scheme stretch visual space.

Convertible and Multipurpose Pieces

What do you think of when you hear the words "convertible furniture?" A creaking sleeper sofa that's hard to pull out and agony upon which to sleep? If so, think again.

Today's convertible and multipurpose furniture now includes not only better-designed and better-looking sleepers but also a slew of other pieces that can do double duty and are a godsend for maximizing small rooms of any kind. Before you start furnishing your small space, make a list of all the activities that will go on there. Then, to optimize function and efficiency, shop for furniture that serves you in multiple ways.

Most furniture manufacturers offer multipurpose pieces in their latest lines. Once you have decided what sort of pieces will meet your needs, visit stores and showrooms, check catalogs, or browse the Internet to see what's available. There's bound to be something that perfectly suits your needs.

Examples of recent introductions include two unusual pieces that look like large trunks when closed; one opens to reveal a single bed with storage in a padded headboard; the other opens to offer a complete, although very compact, home office. Another new piece, a hide-away table and desk, would be ideal for a small living room with a traditional decor. As a side table, the solid-wood piece has a generous top; when it's time to write letters, make a shopping list, or do some other non-computer type work, gently pull the table apart, and you've got a cushioned chair, a small writing surface, and a little drawer. A sleek introduction that's ideal for a space-challenged contemporary room, the "Futaba," designed by Akemi Tanaka, is a streamlined coffee table that can quickly be transformed into a love seat. (For information on furniture manufacturers, see the Resources on page 208.)

In addition, many dining tables, both new designs and old standbys, can be expanded for guests. Drop-leaf tables are especially handy; some of them fold down to almost nothing, then expand in a flash. But to seat a crowd of eight or more you'll probably need a table with separate leaves; these tables expand easily, too, if they're well designed. And there are clever tables of all sizes and shapes—narrow rectangles, squares, ovals—that

LEFT
The homeowner can easily move the coffee table and the demure cane chairs out of the way when this sofa is needed for an overnight guest. Built-in shelves are a smart use of wall space.

serve as occasional pieces, writing desks, or homework centers but convert quickly to accommodate dinner for two, four, or six.

A higher-than-standard coffee table can double for dining, says Lucianna Samu, "Twenty-three inches is a great height." But some new standard-height coffee tables can also do double duty for a casual meal or extra seating. One model, a handsome glass-and-wood piece, comes with comfortable stools that slide under the table when not in use and become part of the design. A similar piece offers a solid wood coffee table with four wood stools that slide in and out. Some new coffee tables also pull up and open out for dining.

Armoires, both new and antique, are often outfitted to hold TVs, additional media equipment, and even mini-bars—all great ideas for small-space entertaining. Mobile furniture is also good in a pinch—a cart on wheels with storage underneath can roll into any room and go to work as a kitchen island, desk, dining table, crafts center, and more.

Convertible and multipurpose pieces don't have to be new. Antique or flea-market trunks or blanket chests can handsomely serve as a coffee table and store table linens or off-season clothes at the same time.

Combined Spaces

People who live in small houses need to think about not only multipurpose furniture but also multifunctional rooms. If you don't have a space you can dedicate solely to guests, think about combining a guest room with a home office. Shop for one of today's new-and-improved sofa beds, one that provides a comfortable mattress and is easy to pull out. A daybed with a trundle bed underneath is another possibility. Use the daybed as a sofa; then slide out the trundle bed when company comes. Or how about a sofa that pulls up instead of out and becomes two comfy bunk beds? There are also easy chairs that open into single beds, so while you're at it, you may as well create a guest room that can sleep two people. Futons are another option, but

test them before buying—they're not all comfortable.

Install your home office—computer, files, supplies, and all—in a cabinet, armoire, or other piece that you can close up when guests arrive. A handsome armoire that holds everything will be much more attractive than a standard desk, even if the desktop is neat and orderly. If you need more storage space for your papers, use one or two drawers in a small bureau, leaving the other drawers empty—and lined with pretty paper—for guests. If there's room, add a boudoir chair, small table, and lamp, and sprinkle the room with family photos for a cozy personal touch.

OPPOSITE TOP
Bookcases and an early nineteenth-century armoire handsomely handle storage in a tiny sitting room.

RIGHT
Strategic multipurpose use of space in this apartment provides a media center, bar, dining area, and sitting area. To unify it all, the custom cabinetry was designed to match the rest of the furniture. Using two small tables for dining instead of one large single piece is another space-saving strategy.

smart tip

QUALITY CHECKS

When shopping for wood furniture you'll find varying levels of quality and pricing. Use this checklist to judge what you're getting for your money.

Frames

- Veneers and laminates should be securely joined to the base material.
- Joints bearing weight should be reinforced with corner blocks.
- Back panels should be screwed into the frame.
- Long shelves should have center supports.

Drawers

- Drawers should fit well, glide easily, and have stops.
- Drawer bottoms should be held by grooves, not staples or nails.
- Drawer interiors should be smooth and sealed.
- Drawer corners should have dovetail joints.

Doors

- Cabinet doors should open and close smoothly.
- Hinges and other hardware should be strong and secure.

Finishes

- All finishes should feel smooth unless they are intentionally distressed or crackled.

design workbook

OPEN, OUTDOOR AMBIANCE

light and airy mood

Many elements work together to open up this long, narrow room—the color scheme creates a fluid, airy feel; tall windows bring in light; and a ceiling fan and potted palm heighten vertical space. A hutch anchors one end, which flows into a sitting area enlivened by tropical-print vintage upholstery and then into the room's dining area (top left).

scaled-down furniture

Small, lightweight tables and chairs that can be easily moved allow for versatility in the furniture layout.

space-saving shapes

Chairs with rounded arms are sensible at tight corners. An oval dining table with leaves, left, takes up less floor space than one with a rectangular shape.

design workbook
STREAMLINED SERENITY

resist over-furnishing

Working with limited square footage, the homeowners made their master bedroom look roomy and inviting by keeping furniture to a minimum.

expand with lines

The rug, with its bold border, and the chair rail bisecting the two wall colors visually elongate the room. The integrated color scheme is another space-stretching strategy.

find furniture that fits

A double dresser just fits against the wall, here, top left. The lesson? Take measurements of walls and furniture pieces before buying.

use tall pieces

A tall chest makes excellent use of vertical space. This one, left, has deep drawers that can accommodate bulky items.

design workbook
COMBINED LIVING SPACES

In a long and narrow New York City apartment, a wall was removed to make a small living room and tiny dining room into a spacious open-plan area. The clean-lined furniture, light-toned woods, and Zen-inspired simplicity enhance the spaciousness. A terra-cotta-color rug mixes in some rich color.

slim seating

A bench pulls up to the dining table for seating, top left. A smart choice for small spaces, it takes up less visual space than chairs yet seats more people. A sky-light spills light into the window-less kitchen area.

easy viewing

An unobtrusive flat-panel TV keeps a traffic aisle open, left.

6

color and pattern

PART SCIENCE, PART ART   PATTERN   THE BOTTOM LINE
DESIGN WORKBOOK

Interior designers refer to color as decorating's most powerful tool. To take that concept a little further, color can be used, like any other tool, to create beauty or wreak havoc. If you slap paint on the walls of your small space or introduce pattern haphazardly, you'll probably end up creating havoc rather than beauty.

In a generously proportioned room, or an especially large one, the choice of a wall color is not crucial to the apparent size of the room. One color may look better than another, of course, and it's possible to choose a truly dreadful one; but even an ill-advised choice will not make one of these rooms look appreciably smaller. In tight quarters, however, color and pattern decisions take on greater importance. The wrong choice could perceptually shrink the space.

LEFT
Against a backdrop of light walls and a pale carpet, some pattern, a bit of texture, and a jolt of energetic color take center stage.

Space-challenged rooms notwithstanding, it is best to consider your house as a whole—like a blank artist's canvas—rather than a series of rooms. Each room will have a character of its own, but unless it is linked to other rooms by architecture, scale and proportion, and color, visual chaos ensues.

The progression from one part of the house to another should be fluid and harmonious with the colors you have chosen, providing visual links that lead the eye serenely. This har-mony doesn't have to be dull—there's always an opportunity for colorful surprises—but the overall effect should be coherent.

Basking in a harmonious palette, your interiors will exude an overall feeling of spaciousness, which in turn will help to make each individual room feel bigger.

According to decorating guru Lynette Jennings, "If you would like the sense of color change or a new scheme as you move from dining area to living area to foyer, for example, work your colors into your upholstery selections and accessories, using the background wall color as the connector." Or, she continues, if your heart is set on using different colors in each room, work within the same color family, using darker or lighter shades as you move through the house.

A white ceiling and cabinets reflect the light while yellow walls cast a glow.

part science, part art

"Color has gotten bolder in the last few years," says interior designer Patricia Gaylor. "I generally opt for serene shades like green or blue, but my customers are now asking for more intense, saturated versions of those colors. There is a definite trend for very bright, hot shades of orange and pink." You have probably seen these ultra-brights lately—and some wild color combinations as well: violet and lime green, for example, or orange and fuchsia. These combinations are so bold that they may seem just casually thrown together. It probably wasn't that spontaneous; the colors work because the person who combined them knew that they were complementary—that is, opposite each other on the color wheel, such as violet and lime green—or next to each other, like orange and fuchsia.

color's vocabulary

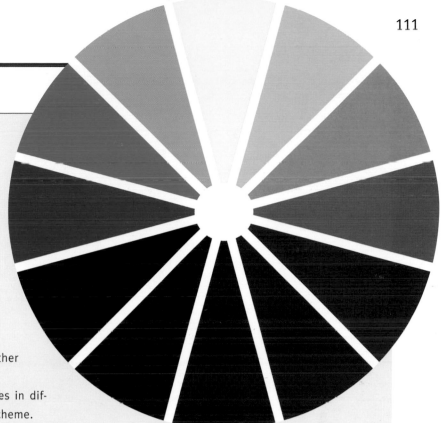

The following terms are used to identify types of colors or explain their interrelationships.

- **Advancing colors:** Warm colors and dark colors, which seem to advance toward you.
- **Analogous colors:** Any three colors located next to one another on the color wheel.
- **Color scheme:** A group of colors used together to create visual harmony.
- **Color wheel:** A circular arrangement of the 12 basic colors that shows how they relate to one another. (See the illustration on this page.)
- **Complementary colors:** Colors located opposite one another on the color wheel.
- **Contrast:** Using colors with different values and intensities in different proportions to create visual harmony in a color scheme.
- **Cool colors:** Greens, blues, and violets.
- **Double-split complementary colors:** The colors located on each side of two complementary colors on the color wheel.
- **Earth tones:** The neutral colors that dominate in nature.
- **Hue:** Synonym for color. Used most often to describe the color family to which a color belongs.
- **Intensity:** The brightness or dullness of a color. Also referred to as a color's purity or saturation.
- **Intermediate colors:** Red-orange, yellow-orange, yellow-green, blue-green, blue-violet, and red-violet; the six colors made by mixing equal amounts of a primary and secondary color.
- **Native colors:** The basic inorganic pigments derived from minerals, used to make the colors found in artist's oil paints.
- **Pastel:** A color to which a lot of white has been added to make it very light in value.
- **Primary colors:** Red, yellow, and blue; the three colors in the visible spectrum that cannot be broken down into other colors. In various combinations and proportions, they make all other colors.
- **Quaternary colors:** Colors made by mixing two tertiary colors.
- **Receding colors:** Cool colors and light colors, which make surfaces seem farther from the eye.
- **Secondary colors:** Orange, green, and violet; the colors made by mixing equal amounts of two primary colors.
- **Shade:** A color to which black has been added to make it darker.
- **Split complementary:** A color paired with the colors on each side of its complementary color.
- **Tertiary colors:** Colors made by combining two secondary colors.
- **Tint:** A color to which white has been added to make it lighter in value.
- **Tone:** A color to which gray has been added to change its value.
- **Triad:** Any three colors located equidistant from one another on the color wheel.
- **Value:** The lightness (tint or pastel) and darkness (shade) of a color.
- **Value scale:** A graphic tool used to show the range of values between pure white and true black.
- **Warm colors:** Reds, oranges, yellows, and browns.

The Science Part

Light reflected through a prism creates a rainbow, known as the color spectrum. Each band of color blends into the next; the longest band is red, then come orange, yellow, green, blue, and violet. Modern color theory takes those bands from the spectrum and forms them into a circle, known as the *color wheel*, to show the relationship of one color to another.

The color wheel includes primary colors (red, blue, and yellow), secondary colors (green, orange, violet), and tertiary colors (red-blue, blue-red, and so on). Secondary colors are made by combining two primaries; a mix of blue and yellow, for instance, makes green. Mixing a primary and a secondary produces a tertiary color—a blue and green mixture makes turquoise.

Colors, or hues, vary in their intensity— that is their level of purity or saturation. The primary, secondary, and tertiary colors are full intensity.

Lightening a color with white produces a *tint*. Darkening it with black creates a *shade*, and if you add gray you arrive at a *tone*.

In addition to altering the intensity of a color, these methods affect what is known as its value, or its lightness or darkness. Tinting gives a color a lighter value and shading creates a darker value.

Take a look at the color wheel and color vocabulary on page 111.

Use both to help you choose and combine colors—and to prevent you from provoking a color war on your walls.

In addition to making walls seem to advance or retreat, color creates mood. So before you pick a pigment, ask yourself—what will I be doing in this room?

RIGHT
Cool green and gray-blue make the walls appear to recede in these adjoining rooms. A special-effects glazed finish gives the green walls an antique look.

smart steps
choosing colors

Step 1 COOL IT

Because they make everyone think of the sea, the sky, and the forest, blue, green, and violet—and their many relatives—are called cool colors. At one end of the spectrum, these colors verge on cold and antiseptic. However, at the other end, blue, green, and even violet become nurturing and comforting.

And because they generally make the walls of a room seem to retreat, they are often chosen to visually expand space.

But don't let their retreating nature fool you—bright blue walls can be just as overwhelming as red ones in a small space, especially if natural light is lacking. And if you feel cramped and claustrophobic, you won't be soothed by the serenity that blue is supposed to exude. Relieving the brightness of blue with white trim and other white accents, however, makes it crisp and fresh, counteracting the cramped feeling; and in its lightest tints, or muted with a touch of gray, blue is both calming and space-enhancing.

Green, the color of nature, is a mixture of blue and yellow. Experts consider the color green to be easy on the eye, with a laid-back, space-enhancing tendency to recede from view. In a small room, a vivid kelly green might draw too much attention to itself, but muted shades such as sage, moss, apple, or forest green can look rich without being intrusive.

Violet in all its guises is a somewhat unconventional choice for a kitchen, dining room, or living area, but in pale tints of lilac and lavender, it's long been a favorite for bedrooms and baths, appreciated for its freshness and its flattering effect on skin tones. And remember— there are no rules. If a strong violet or purple is your heart's desire, you can make it work anywhere. Some designers say, in fact, that regal purple makes a dramatic and effective backdrop for fine antique furniture. Used in its deepest hues, violet will not help your small room look larger, but it will surely make a dramatic and individualistic statement.

Like green, purple is a versatile merging of warm and cool, and by changing the proportions of the mix, you can tip the color into either camp. A purple with lots of red, ranging from light to dark violet-pink, burgundy, or magenta, can be lively and toasty-warm and as sweet as any pink. However, strengthening purple's blue component creates intense violet shades or pale lavender. Both of these colors have an emphatically cool sensibility.

Pastel shades of purple, whether warm or cool, have a definite space-enhancing effect on a room with small dimensions. You may want to try pale purple in a small bedroom, for example. It can look surprisingly formal dressed in white moldings and white furniture.

Step 2 WARM IT UP

You already know that the warm colors of the spectrum—red, yellow, and orange—are lively and stimulating, whether they're used in fashion, the automotive industry, or your living room. Reds are festive, yellows feel cheery, orange is earthy. They all energize the atmosphere of a room.

If you're struggling with a small space, you also need to know that warm colors advance, making the walls seem to come forward and feel closer. This is particularly true of undiluted warm colors. If you're after a cozy look, this color advancement is just what you want. But to effectively open up a small space, consider the array of tints and shades possible with each warm hue.

Red, for example, can be lightened to various luscious shades of pink—cotton-candy pink for a little girl's room, pale warm pink for a bathroom, coral pink for a living area.

Deep, saturated yellow may be too strong indoors, especially in a sunny room, but a little lightening goes a long way, creating a buttermilk tint, a soft lemony

smart tip CONTRAST

"I like to use contrast, especially high contrast, to expand space," says Lucianna Samu, an accomplished interior designer. "A tiny powder room painted dark red with pure white trim and accessories will appear larger. But a duck-egg blue ceiling and warm beige trim will make that same red room feel tinier. Another look that I love—a vivid red room with north-facing windows covered in layers of fabulous white-silk draperies. Now imagine that vivid room with wood plantation shutters." She concludes, "Contrast—that's the answer."

ABOVE

The bold terra-cotta in this sitting room was not chosen to expand visual space but to capitalize on the intimacy of the small space by adding warmth and interest.

RIGHT

In a narrow dining room, a preponderance of neutral colors for the walls, carpet, table, and chairs creates an illusion of greater visual space. Touches of warm reddish-brown rescue the room from blandness.

ABOVE
In this living room, warm, cream-colored walls provide a neutral canvas against which rich colors and complex patterns can be superimposed.

OPPOSITE
Tangerine, once considered a risky color choice for interiors, has now become a "comfort" color, and is showing up more often in activity areas like family rooms and kitchens.

shade, or a yellow so pale it almost qualifies as a neutral. Orange in its purest form would not suit most people's palette preferences, but picture it lightened to a pale peach or softened to delicate orange blossom. These variations will give you the warmth you're seeking and, at the same time, open up space.

Earth tones—terra-cotta, brown, deep red, burnt orange, golden yellow, olive green, to name just a few in this large category—are warm colors in subdued form. Less vivid and more restful than pure red or bright yellow, they resemble the pigments that occur naturally in the earth—various kinds of soil, minerals, and rocks. They are rich but weathered, as though faded by the sun or tempered by the elements, and they offer a welcoming feeling of timelessness and familiarity.

Although less energetic than the undiluted warm colors, earth tones will also appear to pull the walls of a small room closer. If you're seeking snugness, these shades will deliver it. If you're looking for openness, paler earth tones are effective and will give you a warmer look than some neutrals would.

Any of these shades are good choices for kitchens and other public, high-energy rooms. They're inviting, welcoming, and warm. But a space-shrinking shade in a very small kitchen could quickly turn on you, creating claustrophobia and confusion.

In fact, unless you're going for a theatrical effect—which could be very intriguing and successful in a powder room—stay away from deep colors for any very small area. In an entry hall, for example, extra-dark walls will make the space seem cave-like, especially when you enter from a bright or sunny day. If you love those deep earth tones but don't want to lose visual space, go creamier rather than paler.

smart tip UPCOMING TRENDS

Each year, several organizations identify the direction of color trends, which they then "translate" into salable colors for all industries, including products of all kinds for the home—paint, wallcoverings, fabrics, furniture, dishes, kitchen utensils, table-top items, towels, bed linens, and more. According to the Rohm and Haas Paint Quality Institute, today's color Oscars can be divided into three areas:

The allure of comfort foods will pervade interiors as people search for hues that warm and excite. These are Comfort Colors, such as biscuit and wheat naturals, cocoa brown, pumpkin orange, and cinnamon apple pie. These colors, says the Institute, will "wrap your rooms in warmth and promote a stress-free space." And, they say, the comfort-color palette is especially good for kitchens and family rooms.

The Institute thinks that a growing focus on the environment and sustainable products will create an interest in Back to Nature colors such as yellows, blues, leaf-like greens, and organic browns that bring the outdoors inside. And rust or copper-like metallics, they predict, will show up as subtler accent colors. The Institute sees these colors being used in bedrooms and baths or on accent walls in any room.

With a palette of clear reds, deep plums, and sophisticated black and white, the Stark Contrast group is ideal for use as accents or backdrops. Living rooms, dining rooms, or powder rooms are appropriate places for these bold and spicy colors.

Step 3 SHIFT INTO NEUTRAL

Sometimes dismissed as too bland, neutral colors come in a huge array of tones from cool to warm, many of them quite interesting and effective. Strictly speaking, neutrals range from white to black and include all the grays. But for decorating purposes, off-whites, creams, and soft shades of brown such as taupe, beige, and ecru are also considered neutrals, as are certain very subtle shades of other colors.

Like earth tones, neutrals reflect the colors of nature. They have often been relegated to supporting roles in room design, but the richer and more interesting shades can easily stand alone. They effectively enhance and expand the flow of space, and equally important, they provide a low-key backdrop against which you can showcase vividly colored furniture, fabrics, or accessories without making the room feel cramped. That's one of the charms of neutrals—they go with anything, so you can have fun choosing those bold secondary colors. In fact, to keep a neutral palette from looking bland you do need to add touches of color.

For example, if you paint your walls creamy white, choose creamy-white upholstery, and furnish the room in light-toned woods, the room will seem large, but everything in it will seem to disappear. Painting a dark, bulky piece of furniture the same color as the walls can minimize its size. But if all of your furniture disappears, you'll be left with a blank sort of look, like marshmallow sauce on vanilla ice cream.

Step 4 ADD CONTRAST

Paint the wall a deeper shade of a neutral color that is on your furniture. You'll create a more interesting room even if all the other elements remain the same. The wall color will still be light enough to expand space, but the room will be more appealing.

Pairing a neutral hue with pure-white trim will brighten it and bring out its warmth, or combining shades, such as a rich mushroom beige on the walls with paler versions on the ceiling and woodwork, can create surprising richness. And of course, what is as dramatic as white with black accents?

Patricia Gaylor recalls a project she did with architect Sarah Susanka. "She recommended using one neutral color throughout the house and punctuating it with deep tones of red, brown, and gold on end walls,

niches, and behind bookcases. It's a great way to bring in color, and the rich earthy hues were perfect with the neutral walls.

"In another project we did neutral walls in a bedroom but used a bright wall color behind the bed. As a result, the space looks bigger than it actually is but not boring."

Too much contrast can also be a problem, creating an unbalanced, awkward look. For example, if there are several pieces of heavy-looking, dark-wood furniture that you simply must have in your small living room, don't make the mistake of painting the walls around it white or a very light color. In this scenario, the contrast would make the furniture stand out awkwardly. When one handsome piece stands out it gives the room focus; when all of the furniture stands out, the eye

ABOVE

Placed against a white wall, this white bookcase would practically disappear, but with a cream-colored wall behind it, it pops out as an interesting architectural element.

OPPOSITE

Earthy colors, a variety of rich textures, and a comfy couch work together to create an invitation to relax. Mixed with a sure hand, all of the elements coexist in perfect harmony.

doesn't know where to go and chaos results.

In addition to making small rooms look bigger, muted tones, such as creams and beiges, elicit a restful feeling and are ideally suited to bedrooms or baths. Deeper neutrals, such as light browns or grays, don't show dirt and soil as readily as lighter neutrals—they would be good choices for kitchens, family rooms, or other spaces that get a lot of use.

Pure, brilliant white opens up a room effectively but can look harsh unless judiciously paired with other colors. In a kitchen or bathroom, white suggests cleanliness and efficiency, but to circumvent a laboratory-like ambiance, add texture and accent colors. Love the idea of white as a room-expander? Take the edge off with a tinted shade that contains just the slightest hint of peach, pink, or green.

Another advantage to a predominantly neutral scheme is that you can establish a whole new look from time to time simply by changing accessories—in the living room, bring in a colorful slipcover, some pillows, new draperies; in the bedroom, splurge on bright bed linens, curtains, throw rugs; in the bath, make a splash with vivid patterns for towels, rugs, and shower curtain. Almost any color or pattern you choose will succeed.

ABOVE
The lavish use of white brightens and visually enlarges this living room. To maintain the openness, provide contrast, and create design interest, doses of subdued gray and gray-blue are sprinkled throughout.

13 designer techniques

Just as color has the power to produce physical and emotional changes, it also has the ability to visually mold space. It influences perceptions of size and shape, masks flaws, highlights good points, and creates harmony throughout a house.

1   To alter a room's physical size, paint it a light, cool color to make it seem a bit larger and airier; a dark or warm color will make it seem smaller as well as cozier.

2   To warm north- or east-facing rooms, which tend to be cool and receive weak natural light, decorate them with light or bright and warm colors. To temper south-facing rooms, which tend to get hot (particularly in summer), or west-facing rooms, which are bright and warm (especially on summer afternoons), decorate with light, cool colors.

3   To raise a room's visual height, carry the wall color to the ceiling. Paint any crown or cove molding the same color as the walls.

4   To make a high ceiling appear lower or make a room feel more intimate, stop the wall's color 9 to 12 inches below the ceiling, and accent that line with a stenciled border, a wallpaper border, or molding. An alternative technique is to paint the ceiling with a subdued accent shade, bringing it onto the wall 9 to 12 inches below the ceiling line. Then accent the line with a border.

5   To coordinate a room completely, tint white ceiling paint slightly with a bit of the wall color.

6   To camouflage an unsightly feature, such as a radiator, paint it the same color as the walls.

7   To highlight an attractive feature such as a paneled door, paint it a color that contrasts with the walls.

8   To provide control in a room decorated with bright, bold colors or many different colors, paint the woodwork, ceiling, and other architectural features white.

9   To successfully paint your walls a dark or intense color, finish the project by sealing them with a non-yellowing clear top coat to magnify their depth and reflect light. This final step is especially important in small or dark rooms.

10 To unify a house with all-white or all-beige walls, use the same shade in all of the rooms.

11 To create harmony throughout a house, choose a signature color, and use it in some way in each room. Make it the dominant color in one room, the secondary color in another, the accent color in a third, an accessory color in a fourth, and so on.

12 To unify a house in which different hues have been used in each room, use neutral colors in transitional spaces such as hallways. This not only visually separates spaces but also prevents color clashes between rooms.

13 To keep decorative paint finishes from clashing where they meet, use the same technique to execute them, even if they contain different colors.

pattern

When it comes to pattern, conventional wisdom issues a couple of directives—one, don't use it on the walls in a small room; two, if you absolutely must use it, choose a small-scale design in one or two colors with plenty of white in the background. This is good advice, as far as it goes. There are plenty of good-looking small-scale wall-covering patterns available, and you can't go wrong using one of them in your small space.

But you can also break this rule—as you can defy conventional wisdom on the use of color—and enliven the walls with a bold or exuberant large-scale pattern. Having broken the first rule, however, you need to obey a couple of others to make it all work. First, restrict yourself to one pattern; without the sure hand of a professional designer, it's tricky to introduce a second pattern into a small room, even if it's close to the primary one in color and design. The visual chaos you create could chop up the

visual harmony of your space and make it look even smaller. Second, take care that furniture, floors, rugs, and other large elements repeat or complement, rather than compete with, the hues in the pattern you have chosen. To avoid the dreaded design chaos, you should unify the overall look of the room by coordinating the various elements as much as possible.

If you lack confidence in your ability to mix patterns, check out the books in your local home center or wallcovering store. Working with design professionals, manufacturers provide an abundance of coordinated wallcovering and fabric collections that take the guesswork out of mixing and matching.

Large-scale, bold patterns, like warm colors, seem to advance, moving the walls toward you. Used in a small room, they will not visually expand space, but if they are handled skillfully, they will create a lively look or a cozy, intimate atmosphere. If you're smitten with an exuberant design that you feel you must use but are afraid it will overwhelm the room, restrict it to a sin-

gle wall, which allows you to inject design interest without creating chaos or feeling, says Patricia Gaylor, "like you're trapped inside a gift-wrapped box."

Lavishly patterned walls can be stylish and effective in dining rooms, living rooms, and if the colors are restful, bedrooms. In kitchens, bold patterns may prove too busy. In bathrooms, where a serene soak in the tub is often the goal, they may provide too much distraction.

No one stays very long in a tiny powder room, which is why it's the perfect place to go a little wild with design drama and ovrt-the-top glamour. "In a very small room, pattern really looks good," says Gaylor. "I love doing phone-booth-sized powder rooms in a lot of pattern. In one, my decorative painter and I covered all the walls, even the door, in a forest mural. You don't feel claustrophobic because you're too busy looking at all the cool stuff on the walls."

If you'd rather not take a walk on the wild side, follow con-

OPPOSITE

Don't let a small-space challenge force you to give up lively patterns altogether. In this small bedroom, a toile print on a pumpkin-colored ground is restricted to one wall. Harmonious colors for the other walls, ceiling, and bed linens pull it together.

BELOW

Occasionally, vivid, lively patterns work successfully in a small space, particularly if the design is small and there's plenty of white in the background. A case in point is the wallcovering and matching fabric shown here.

RIGHT

In an otherwise neutral room, even a small one, you can safely give expression to your love of energetic color and pattern, limiting it to small doses here and there. In this room, the brick hearth, rattan chair, and nubby rug add texture.

ventional wisdom and cover the walls of your space-challenged rooms in a small-scale print with a generous amount of light- or medium-toned color as the ground. Some small-scale wallcoverings are neat and orderly, with a slightly dignified and formal look, nice additions for traditionally styled living rooms, dining rooms, studies, home offices, or even kitchens. Jauntier prints could add pizzazz to a country kitchen, a family bath, or a kid's room, and pretty, delicate florals are just right for bedrooms.

Fabric Prints

You could also stick to paint for the walls and introduce pattern via upholstery fabrics, slipcovers, curtains, carpets, rugs, and accessories. And if you have chosen a wall color that makes the room seem larger, you've got plenty of leeway to get creative with patterned fabrics without compromising the visual flow.

Generally, experts advise using large prints on large pieces of furniture, medium prints on medium pieces, and small prints on accent pieces. Keeping in mind the principles of scale and proportion you can see that a large-scale pattern looks better on a sofa than it does on a dining room chair; similarly, a delicate stencil is more appropriate as a border on a tabletop than as a border on a wall.

Another trick for mixing patterns is to provide links of scale, motif, and color. The regularity of checked, striped, and geometric patterns—particularly if they are small-scale and low-contrast—makes them easy to mix. A small floral can play off a thin ticking stripe, while a cabbage-rose chintz may require a bolder stripe to create a same-scale mix.

When putting patterns together, take into account the nature of the fabric. A formal silk or damask fabric is a shock to the senses paired with a casual gingham or a nubby cotton, but damask and moiré are good partners, as are gingham and ticking stripes.

The most effective link is shared colors or a similar level of intensity between the prints. Make sure all of your patterns contain at least one hue that is similar, even if it's a background or neutral color. Exact matches are the backbone of manufacturers' coordinated fabric-and-wallcovering collections, but to create your own personal mix, interpret that approach loosely and experiment to see which pattern combinations work for you.

the bottom line

In general the rule seems to be that neutrals, cool tones, or pale versions of deeper colors can expand visual space in a small room—and simple patterns with a light background enhance that effect. This is a perfectly good time-honored "rule." But that doesn't mean you have to follow it. You may want more than the illusion of greater space from your small rooms; you may also want comfort, livability, and practicality.

So if it suits you, throw away the rule book and pick your favorite color—whether it be plum, forest green, or cocoa brown, keeping in mind all of the other space-expanding advice you've been given. Because in the end, size is irrelevant in a beautiful room that makes you feel happy and at home.

OPPOSITE

Soft-beige painted walls qualify as a neutral in this diminutive bedroom. The design interest here comes from the cheerful patterned window shade, the checked comforter, and the floral pillows, all of which can be changed quickly and easily.

ABOVE

To make a good-looking architectural feature stand out, contrast it with the walls and furniture surrounding it. Here a nineteenth-century carved mantel was given a couple of coats of glossy-white paint to make it pop against the deep coral-color wall behind it.

design workbook
BRIGHTEN A BUNGALOW

pattern pizzazz

Against walls of neutral color and a wealth of natural materials, pattern revs up a small seaside cottage. United by color and scale, the patterns brighten the furniture and window hangings. Slipcovers unzip easily for washing or a quick change to another pattern. Beachy textures include rattan chairs, a sisal rug, and bamboo blinds.

compact but cozy

The conversation area is small but comfy, top left. Bamboo blinds slide down when privacy is needed. When they're open, in streams daylight, and the narrow room feels spacious.

a space-saving plan

To emphasize visual height, left, the ceiling is white; painted a contrasting color, the end gable also draws the eye up. For meals, the owners use a space-saving counter that borders a kitchen.

design workbook

AN ATTIC OASIS

mellow yellow

Sunny-yellow wall paint and a mellow wood floor unite all parts of this open-plan attic apartment, creating a smooth visual flow that makes the space look larger. Offset by white furniture and curtains, the color looks especially crisp and refreshing. A tiny but efficient eat-in kitchen occupies the rear corner of the apartment.

a touch of red

A fabric-covered folding screen divides the sleeping and living areas, top left. The vivid red toile comforter introduces an accent color and looks cozy on a small bed tucked under the eaves.

double-duty table

When the owner gives a dinner party, her refectory table seats up to eight comfortably. At other times, left, she pushes it against the wall to save floor space and uses it for crafts.

storage

CONQUERING CLUTTER   SEEKING STORAGE   DESIGN WORKBOOK

There are a couple of theories circulating about home storage space: one, there isn't enough of it; two, there never can be enough of it. It seems that most people believe that no matter the size of their house —and how efficient the storage system appears to be—things accumulate and so does the need for more storage.

Neither of these theories is true, provided that you stay on top of the issues of clutter and storage. Especially when your space is small, staying on top becomes even more important. One of the keys to successful small-space living is keeping it simple, which is not really possible if there is too much stuff. Another key to home comfort, in general, is putting function first, knowing that all else will fall into place. So before you even approach storage, face the clutter challenge.

LEFT
Great-looking containers, such as these baskets, are handy for corralling clutter in any room of the house.

The most efficient storage system possible will not help you for very long if you have not purged your home of clutter and adopted a healthy attitude that will keep it from accumulating again. You can do this important job yourself, inspired by advice that you'll read here. Or you can hire a professional to do it for you. A natural outgrowth of the massive cultural changes since the 1970s and the busy lives most people live today, these pros are variously called space planners, professional organizers, or closet specialists. Answering an apparently large need, there are several organizations that represent these specialists. The National Association of Professional Organizers (NAPO), for instance, has several thousand members who teach clients organizing skills and principles.

Working with both residential and business clients, professional organizers focus on such areas as filing systems and paper management; home offices; closets; kitchens; attics, garages, and basements. Some come to your home and do hands-on organizing, helping you to sort through every item and decide what to do with it, then creating systems to help you stay clutter free.

To find an organizer in your area you can check out NAPO or the Professional Organizers Web Ring, which have Web sites that are easy to find on the Internet. Just do a search of "professional organizers" or just "organizers;" check the Yellow Pages under the same heading; or seek recommendations from friends and neighbors who may have used these services.

There is no official course of training for professional organizers, and although affiliation with an association shows serious intent, it does not guarantee competence. When hiring, you should look for prior work experience in related fields, such as office management; ask to see a portfolio of completed jobs (or the jobs themselves); get some business references; and ask to talk to at least three previous clients, asking the pertinent questions suggested on page 17, in Chapter 1.

coming to terms with clutter

Clutter clings, says feng shui consultant Stephanie Roberts, for two reasons. One, you may be too distracted by your busy life to deal with it. That's simple to fix. Two, you may actually avoid dealing with it for emotional reasons. That's not so simple. "Running unprepared into the not-so-simple aspects of clutter can bring all of our good intentions to a halt," warns Roberts.

Here are some of the problem areas Roberts identifies. Do any of them sound familiar?
- Clothes that don't fit anymore. Letting go of them means accepting your current weight and your level of physical fitness— or lack of it.
- An expensive item you never use. Getting rid of it means admitting that you made a poor choice when you bought it.
- Books or magazines you've never read. Purging these items, says Roberts, requires you to face the fact that you "will never have enough time or attention to explore every topic that's of interest to you."

Rather than face these tough truths, you pass over the never-worn clothes and never-read magazine in a haze of denial. But, Roberts claims, you'll never clear the decks if you don't come to terms with the emotional discomfort certain kinds of clutter cause. Certain ideas can help you let go, she says:
- The past is over and the future isn't here. But confronting the emotions raised by clutter will make life in the present more peaceful.
- As you become more aware of what kinds of things you have held onto, you'll learn to make better choices about what you bring into your home. People who can live without clutter trust themselves to make good choices.
- Do the best you can, Roberts suggests. If your emotions get in the way you won't be able to get rid of all your clutter at once. But each time you tackle it you'll probably be able to let go of a little more. Keep at it, she says, letting go of excess makes room for blessings of all kinds.

conquering clutter

The word "clutter" has a couple of meanings. One definition—and the most common—defines it as "things you don't need, use, or like." Another describes clutter as "anything that is disorganized, untidy, or unfinished." And a definition that is apropos to the topic at hand calls it "too many things in too small a space."

If getting rid of clutter were easy, it wouldn't be a problem for so many of us, and a whole field of expertise would not have grown up around it. Sure, some clutter will yield to a determined attitude and a few hours' work—it's pretty easy to throw out week-old newspapers, torn dish towels, socks with holes in them, and chipped or cracked china, for example. But there are other items that resist all attempts to purge, and these items can really clog your closets, your minds, and your small rooms, keeping you from the airy spacious atmosphere you crave.

Baby Boomers—whose parents lived through the Depression and World War II and preached "don't be wasteful"—may have trouble throwing out things, especially items that are still even a little bit useful. My father

fixed everything that broke or was in danger of wear. Only as a last, desperate resort would he replace an item. I still have a pastry brush with a handle that my father constructed out of a wire hanger. The bristles are a bit stiff, but I can't get rid of it, partly because it's sentimental, and partly because I hear his voice saying, "It works fine—you don't need a new one." Another phrase that stands between many people and freedom from clutter—"It might come in handy someday." (See the sidebar, "Coming to Terms with Clutter," on the previous page.)

Insights about why people cling to clutter may enlighten you and help you to let go. But you don't necessarily have to go into therapy to figure out why you're holding on. Do the best you can and find a space to stow the stuff you can't toss—yet—so that it isn't cramping your style or your space-challenged rooms.

Not everyone has emotional issues about clutter. If you're one of the lucky ones, you can probably grit your teeth and do it. Here are some ideas for how to go about it.

RIGHT
Built-in shelves can forestall any potential storage disaster, even in a potting area. Here, the shelves keep vases, pots, and other essentials orderly and easy to reach.

smart steps
lighten up

Step 1 STAY CALM

Beware of feverish de-cluttering, the experts say. This happens when the situation suddenly seems intolerable and you launch into a frenzy of activity, putting things away, moving piles around, filling half a trash bag with a variety of stuff.

This method never works. Because your activity is frantic, you'll wear yourself out before you accomplish anything. It's like going to the gym for the first time in six months and doing too much—you'll ache so badly that you'll never want to go back. And because you have no overall plan, you haven't really rid yourself of clutter—it will continue to pour in, along with confusion and frustration.

Step 2 MAKE A PLAN

Don't try to do the job all at once. The clutter in your home accumulated over time, and you'll get rid of it the same way, bit by bit.

Schedule regular de-cluttering sessions, even if they're only 15 minutes long. Even better, says Cynthia Townley Ewer, editor of OrganizedHome.com, an on-line magazine, schedule bigger blocks of time, from, say, two to four hours a week for maximum effectiveness.

"Scheduling de-clutter sessions brings the goal out of the stratosphere and into real life," says Ewer. "By committing time to de-cluttering, you strengthen motivation and embrace the goal of a clutter-free home...you begin to create islands, then peninsulas, then continents of de-cluttered space."

Step 3 SELECT A STRATEGY

Clutter is a common problem in today's households, and advice abounds on how to deal with it. One of the most popular methods is the four-box approach. It's simple—find four large boxes or cartons and label them "put away," "give away or sell," "store," and "throw away."

Take the boxes to the room you're de-cluttering. Pick up every item of clutter and consign it to the correct box. Chase down clutter in every storage area in the

room. Cynthia Townley Ewer kicks it up a notch by adding, "You may not release your grip on any item until you have made a decision."

After you have gone through one room, or one section of a room, distribute the contents of the boxes. "Put away" items go back into the closets, drawers, or cabinets where they belong. The "give away or sell" box goes in the trunk of your car if you plan to give it away; from there you can drop it off at a local charity. If you plan to sell items from this box at a future yard sale, set aside an area of your garage for this box and the ones that will follow. Put the "store" box in your

LEFT
In this small kitchen, every square inch of space has been put to work for storage, including the pass-through, which boasts an overhead rack for glasses. Because they are see-through, the glasses don't block sightlines Into the next room.

TOP AND BOTTOM RIGHT
To win the battle against clutter, get creative with space that would otherwise go unused. In an entry hall, top, a single shelf and a row of pegs take care of tote bags, books, and odds and ends. A bench built into a small recess, bottom, is also handy for storage.

basement, attic, or other household storage area. Finally, dump the "throw away" box in the trash—and don't look back.

You can use the four-box method to clear off a single shelf or drawer, or to de-clutter the whole house in a weekend. Forcing a decision will serve you well as you cull clutter from your house, says Ewer.

Of course if you've got storage space—such as an attic, basement or garage—you don't need to be concerned with overall clutter. You can just hide it away and deal with it later—or never. But don't underestimate the negative effect it can have on a small room.

seeking storage

Once you have dealt with the useless odds and ends you may have hoarded, you can begin to devise effective storage strategies for whatever remains. No matter how ruthless you were with your clutter, you're not home free. In every room there are items, specific to the function of that room, that need to be stored: books and magazines in the living room; home-entertainment paraphernalia in the family room; clothes in the bedroom; and so on. The list, unfortunately, is endless.

This is not to recommend excessive neatness. It's unrealistic, difficult to maintain, and tedious for everyone—and, in fact, in any healthy, well-adjusted household there is bound to be a certain amount of clutter. But if things begin to pile up, that claustrophobic feeling is likely to take over your small rooms again. Instead, devise an effective storage system for each room, one that designates a place for everything and allows you to get at whatever you need when you need it. Enlist family members to help.

smart tip   EASY WINDOW SEAT

Not blessed with a bay window, dormer, or other natural location for a window seat? Never mind. You can create a comfy little recess on any wall with a window in it by using standard kitchen cabinets. First, enlist a couple of over-the-refrigerator units or a 42-in.-long drawer to serve as the seat. On either side of the seat, install two tall pantry units—voila!—you've got a cozy nook. Add a thick cushion and a couple of pillows for comfortable seating. Home centers carry stock cabinets, the most economical option; you can also order custom units, which are more expensive but do offer a better selection. In either case, match the door style, finish, and hardware to other elements in the room.

ABOVE LEFT
Instead of consigning this old hutch to a garage sale, the owners spiffed it up with paint and converted it into an entry-hall storage piece for hats, gloves, scarves, and other winter wear.

OPPOSITE
If cabinets in the kitchen are already chock full, find a place in another part of the house for items that you don't use often. Here, in a basement laundry area, a built-in cupboard stores the "good" china, and drawers hold fancy tablecloths and napkins.

Built-in Storage

Built-ins do a lot more than provide storage—they can also provide design interest in any of your rooms. Picture, for example, a small den or sitting room, made cozy and warm, in spite of its limited size, by a handsome wall of bookshelves. Or a living room gaining architectural presence with shelves tucked into the recesses on either side of a fireplace. Even a dining room can take on an air of distinction with shelves full of books and pretty pieces of china. If you don't have a separate dining room, perhaps you can line one wall of your kitchen eating area with built-ins to hold, and display, the china that you use daily.

And because they are so often literally "built in" to exist-ing niches, recesses, dormers, and around or between two windows, they take advantage of space that would not otherwise be used and they consume less floor area than large pieces of storage furniture, such as bulky cabinets or large armoires.

When we think of built-ins, bookshelves come immediately to mind, but don't forget other such useful types as window seats, platform beds with drawers underneath, headboards fitted with handy shelves and compartments, and of course, cabinets.

To decide what type of built-ins you might need—and how many—take a look at what's left after your satisfying purge of clutter and think about what you'll want to display or hide.

Check out the family room. Are individual pieces of electronic equipment scattered all over—TVs, DVD and CD players,

speakers, and so forth? Consolidate them in one built-in wall unit that features both open shelves and closed compartments. Hiding these high-tech elements is particularly important in a room that features a traditional or period decor.

Maybe books are a problem in the living room, stacked on every available surface and making the room look disorganized. Bookshelves are the perfect solution, and if they're built into existing recessed spaces, so much the better for a tight area.

In the bedroom an over-abundance of clothes chests may be eating up precious floor space. A floor-to-ceiling unit with drawers and cupboards would solve that problem nicely, as would a custom-built bed that includes storage drawers. And don't forget the Murphy bed. A time-honored space-saver at its peak of popularity in the 1920s and 30s, it is making a comeback and is available these days in twin, double, queen, and king sizes. In addition to the handy pull-down bed, you can order Murphy wall units that offer shelves, drawers and cupboards for storage, an ideal solution for studio apartments, tiny guest rooms, or home offices that double as guest rooms.

Built-in bunk beds are good space-savers in kids' rooms; for one-child rooms, loft beds are even better. Kids seem to like both aspects of the loft bed—the top for sleeping and the cozy area "hidden" underneath for studying or playing games.

Your storage requirements and the status of your budget will determine the size and complexity of the built-ins you chose, and the style of your rooms will determine their look.

The priciest units are custom-crafted and finished by a cabinetmaker, who painstakingly designs and measures them to fit the exact dimensions of the available space. Ready-made units are also widely available in many sizes, configurations, and price ranges; some units are pre-finished, others are constructed of raw wood that you paint or stain at home. You can spice up fea-

OPPOSITE
Thanks to a wall of built-ins, one section of a dining room in a New York City apartment can also function as a little sitting room or study. The shelves add character to an otherwise featureless wall.

ABOVE
We want all of our media equipment to be easily accessible but don't always like looking at it. One homeowner solved that design dilemma by shielding these entertainment-center shelves with an interesting found object—a fanciful metal gate salvaged from a demolished church.

tureless prefab units by trimming them with moldings or hardware that blend with other pieces in the room. "Closed shelving is best," says Southern California designer Sunday Hendricksen, "otherwise it all tends to look too busy. But if you do use open shelves, paint a color on the wall behind them to hold the area together and give it organization."

Kitchen cabinets are also a source worth investigating. Shop home centers and cabinet showrooms for modules that match the size of the space you have, then pop them right in— it's easy and they'll present a handsome finished look.

Another option is to start from scratch and create the built-ins yourself. Straightforward bookshelves or bookcases are easy do-it-yourself jobs, but it takes a skilled carpenter to put together a platform bed or a complex wall unit.

Finally, choose built-ins that blend with the overall design of the room. For a traditional, somewhat formal space you might go for mellow woods, decorative details, and fancy hardware. In country-style rooms, simple pieces with little adornment are appropriate; you can stain the built-ins, paint them white, or choose a cheerful color that blends with fabrics or other pieces in the room. For contemporary settings, choose clean-lined and unadorned natural wood, metal, or glass pieces.

Contained Storage

"Clutter is space-enemy Number One," says interior designer Lynette Jennings, "and it will fight that spacious feeling you've worked so hard to create." Therefore, even though built-ins are now organizing much of your potential clutter, there are smaller items that also need attention. This is where containers enter the picture.

In a well-organized room there are containers of two types—public and private. "Public" containers hold items that we use often, keeping them organized and easy to access. In the living room or family room, items that need to be tamed include remote controls for media equipment, magazines, or newspapers; in entries or mudrooms, it's coats, gloves, boots, and more; in home offices, it's paper, folders, and supplies. Bedrooms may also benefit from containers that hold remotes, books, and other small items. And in kids' rooms, which famously resist any attempts at order, containers are a must.

Whether they are baskets, boxes, or bins, our public containers are on display while they do their work. Whether you put them on a corner of a large table, place them on the floor in front of the fireplace, or slide them under the coffee table, they should look good, be light enough to move, and harmonize with the

closet control

- Build shelves all the way to the ceiling. Stack the highest, hard-to-reach ones with suitcases, out-of-season clothes, and other items you don't need often.
- If your closet has a little floor space to spare, beef up its storage capacity by adding an inexpensive chest of drawers; even a fiberboard or plastic one will do the job adequately.
- Install two rows of rods—the upper one for blouses and jackets; the bottom one for skirts and pants.

overall style of the room. That's easy to accomplish. Baskets look good almost everywhere; once used predominantly in cutesy, country decors, they are now widely available in sleeker forms that fit well even in contemporary rooms. Coated-wire baskets are appropriate for contemporary or transitional decors, and handsome wooden boxes, antique, reproduction, or brand new, add character as well as storage space to a living room or home office. In kids' rooms, colorful plastic bins are ideal.

"Private" containers stow the stuff we don't need to get at often—table linens, off-season clothes, blankets, extra sheets or towels. In limited space, we may not have the luxury of storing

smart tip SPACE UNDER THE STAIRS

The unused space under a staircase is just begging for built-ins or closed storage. Depending on the size of the area, you can use it for a closet, a set of shelves, a little desk area; you can even build in some stock kitchen or bath cabinets for closed-door storage or add a bench with a storage drawer under it.

A word to the wise: consult an architect or remodeling contractor before you start rearranging space—you might be about to compromise a load-bearing wall or post.

does your closet measure up?

To help you plan an optimally functioning clothes closet, here are the standard lengths (in inches, measured from the pole) for hanging everyday garments. If you are taller than average, be sure to raise the pole a bit higher so that garments won't graze the floor.

Men's Clothing		Women's Clothing	
Pants, folded	32	Bathrobe	52
Pants, unfolded	48	Blouse	36
Shirt	38	Dress	58
Suit	40	Evening gown	69
Ties, folded	32	Skirt	35
Topcoat	56	Suit	37
Winter coat	55	Winter coat	52

ABOVE
Frosted-glass sliding doors reduce the bulky look of a closet that was built into the corner of a bedroom.

OPPOSITE LEFT
Under a flat-screen TV, a long streamlined cabinet holds media equipment and a multitude of other things. Painting it almost the same color as the wall helped to minimize its size.

OPPOSITE RIGHT
In a small room, convertible furniture is a must. This coffee table doubles as a storage chest.

these things in closets or other out-of-the way places. This is where double-duty furniture comes to the rescue. Trunks of various kinds can serve as a coffee table in the living room or an occasional table in the bedroom, holding a lamp, some books, a vase of flowers—and cleverly containing seldom-used items at the same time. Other double-duty pieces that work in any room include storage ottomans that act as foot rests, tables, storage, or extra seating, and large wooden boxes with lift-off lids that can serve as end tables.

Other private containers are the boxes and bins you can push under the bed, stow on the floor or top shelf of a closet, or, as Sunday Hendricksen suggests, slide under a skirted table. For efficiency, these containers should be neat and tidy but it's not so important that they be good looking or blend with the room decor. However, some decorative boxes, such as fabric-covered ones in coordinated prints and various sizes, are pretty enough to put on display.

Finally, here's a couple of tips from the experts: one, label all closed containers so that you know exactly what's inside; two, don't choose a container that will be too heavy to lift after you've filled it.

Closet Storage

Sure, we'd all like huge walk-in closets that practically organize themselves. But unless your home was built in the last 20 or 30 years, your closets are probably small, scarce, and outfitted with a single pole and a shelf that's too high to reach. This is a challenge in any household, but if the rooms in your home are small, it's especially perplexing.

Fortunately, you can overcome the curse of the small closet. Home centers and storage-specialty shops offer a wide range of components—racks, dividers, double hanging bars, and drawers, to name just a few. These components are especially helpful in bedroom closets but can also be tailored to other parts of the house for all kinds of storage needs. Super-organized closets do more than just store clothes and other items; they also eliminate the need for big, bulky pieces of furniture—or lots of little pieces—that eat up floor space and make your small rooms feel crowded and claustrophobic.

The components that organize children's closets are often colorful or whimsical, which, experts believe, make it more likely that the kids will be willing to use them to hang up clothes and put away shoes.

In outfitting kids' closets, place the components within easy reach and choose adjustable poles and shelves that you can move as the little ones grow. Hooks are easy for kids to use, but beware of installing sharp ones, especially at their eye level.

Using readily available kits, most of which offer rods, shelves, coated wire bins, and other components, you can create a closet system that is tailor-made to your specific needs in any room of the house. If this task seems beyond your abilities, or if you want a more custom installation, you can hire a designer or professional organizer to do it for you. Home centers or special-

ty stores often have in-house consultants; or you can also find one by looking on-line, reading the Yellow Pages, or asking friends for recommendations.

Whether you hire a pro or do it yourself, do your closet homework first. Leaf through magazines, catalogs, and books, tearing out photos that inspire you. Do you want sliding or hinged doors? Solid or louvered? Box-style drawers or baskets? Will you want special racks for shoes, segmented compartments for small items, sets of shelves for folded clothes?

Storage that really works for you and your family goes a long way to simplifying your small spaces and making them look airy and open. If you find it difficult to tackle the closet clutter with an objective eye, hiring a pro to organize it for you may be well worth the investment.

smart tip

SLIM DOWN BUILT-INS

To maximize visual space in a small room and reduce the bulky look of a built-in wall unit, make the center section slightly deeper than the units on either side. For example, in a family-room wall unit an 18- to 24-inch center section could hold a TV and other media equipment while two 12-inch-deep sections flanking it would be deep enough for books.

OPPOSITE
Don't overlook any storage possibility. Here, combining variegated drawers with open storage is a smart use of an awkward space.

LEFT
Teaching kids to put their stuff away is easier when storage in their bedrooms is easy to reach. A series of open shelves helps organize the occupant of this cheery playroom. Sliding doors close the noisy space off from adult sections of the apartment.

ABOVE
In the same apartment, a bedroom for older children uses shadow-box-style storage to hold books and toys at eye level.

design workbook
WORK CENTER AND GUEST ROOM

office max

The renovation of the attic turned this space into an airy guest room and home office, despite the pitch of the roof. The clean-lined work table and vertical-stripe wallcovering on the end walls maximize the illusion of taller space. (See also bottom left.)

sleek storage

File cabinets and open shelves keep office essentials handy. Containers of various sizes are key to the orderly, uncluttered look of the room. (See also top left.)

guest quarters

On the far side of the room (left), a sleek couch piled with patterned pillows converts to a comfy bed for guests. To expand the space visually, the owners hung a round mirror to reflect and magnify light from the window opposite, and selected a neutral color scheme.

design workbook

OPENED TO THE RAFTERS

a lofty idea

In an inspired makeover, the owners opened the ceiling above their daughter's tiny bedroom to create a loft storage and study area for her in the attic. A ladder provides access; an antique table performs as a desk; and rustic baskets supply storage. A closet in the hallway provides extra utility space.

cute collectibles

A beam that was exposed in the remodeling is now a display of miniature furniture, top left, but it could be used for other collectibles.

girlish charm

In lieu of a closet and keeping with the vintage charm of the room, an old wooden dresser refreshed with white paint, left, offers additional closed storage.

8

lighting

AT HOME WITH LIGHTING   THE RIGHT BULB   YOUR LIGHTING NEEDS
ROOM BY ROOM   LIGHT TRICKS   DESIGN WORKBOOK

Adequate levels of light are important in any room of your house. Planned correctly, good lighting provides safety and makes interiors look attractive, welcoming, and sometimes, more spacious than they actually are. Good lighting is particularly important when physical dimensions are tight. The uncomfortable, cramped feeling you get in a room that seems too small can be alleviated by a comprehensive lighting plan that incorporates multiple sources, both natural and artificial. Attracting more daylight through windows—existing, enlarged, or additional ones—will make your space-challenged home more functional and generally more pleasant in which to live. And you'll receive additional benefits if you carefully address all of your supplemental lighting needs, both general and specific. Here are some helpful ideas.

LEFT
In a city apartment, recessed fixtures provide overall light. With the fixtures dimmed, table lamps shed a soft glow.

at home with lighting

The field of lighting for the home has come a long way in recent decades. Most people have moved beyond using just a few table lamps in the living room, a bright overhead light in the kitchen, and rows of "Hollywood" lights on either side of the bathroom vanity. These days, lighting specialists plan skillful schemes that are both practical and decorative, enhancing a home's function and showing off its best architectural features, colors, furniture, and textures to advantage.

The amount and of light with which you live, and its color, also affects your sense of well-being. Experts claim that people work well and learn more effectively in bright, warm light. And everyone knows that dim light is restful and relaxing.

Light can also affect your perception of space—directing light upward makes a low ceiling feel taller; washing the walls with light makes a small room seem bigger. A good plan will include available natural light and several types of artificial light for each room in the house.

Natural Exposure

In a recent lecture, Marilyne Andersen of MIT's Department of Architecture puts it succinctly. "Natural light is part of our biological needs," she says. "Intuitively we prefer it to electric light." The experts agree with her. To the human eye, they say, the desirable norm is sunlight. Part of its appeal is its variety—the clear illumination on a cloudless mountaintop, the diffused light of a misty morning, and the intense brightness of a tropical beach. And there are differences, too, between the look of sunlight on a cool rainy morning, a bright summer day, and a crisp and clear winter afternoon. The quality of sunlight also changes as the day moves on—contrast the color of sun at noon, for example, with the way it looks near evening.

BELOW

A sunspace addition brightens a living room and home office. Shades can be drawn over the glass ceiling panels to control heat buildup.

OPPOSITE

Translucent panels on a sunny window create a glare-free surface for this desk. Installed on a track, the panels can be moved as needed.

smart tip

WORKING IN DAYLIGHT

The natural light that streams into a room will affect the tasks that you perform there. Try not to place a desk or work table so that it faces directly into bright sunlight. Conversely, when doing close work avoid turning your back on a window and creating shadows on the work surface. When reading or doing paperwork, arrange the room so that the light falls over your left shoulder.

The amount and quality of natural light that a room receives depend on the size and position of its windows and their orientation to the sun. East-facing rooms get the morning sun. Rooms that are oriented to the west are sunniest in the afternoon. This light can be hot and harsh, so it's important to provide shading for windows with a western exposure. A southern exposure gets sunlight for most of the day. This is ideal for solar heating during the winter, but southern windows must be shielded from summer sun. Northerly rooms, which in essence have their backs to the sun, receive only indirect light and tend to be cool—cold, in fact, in the winter. But north light is diffuse and good for doing close work of various kinds. Artists typically choose studios that are abundant with northern light.

Chapter Two suggests capturing more daylight by enlarging existing windows or adding new ones that could make your rooms look and feel larger. Before you undertake a project such as this, evaluate the existing space—will you use the room year-round, whatever the seasons? What times of the day will you be in the room? What is the orientation of the existing windows in the space? Larger windows won't necessarily make a small, dark room brighter and feel larger. If the existing windows are sited toward the north, for example, expanding their size won't significantly increase available light, and it will very likely make the room feel colder. You can create an airy, cheerful ambiance in a tiny breakfast nook by adding an east-facing window, but don't try to take a late-afternoon nap in a room with beefed-up west-facing windows, unless you can control the bright light with sun-blocking shades or blinds.

So, you see it's important to evaluate the quality of the natural light you will be attracting. The strong light of a bright sunny day creates both light and dark areas and can form harsh shadows. In winter, this light may look especially harsh and may even leach the color out of the room and make it appear flat. The softer light of a cloudy day is diffuse, smooth, and even. It creates very few shadows or intense bright spots.

In general, early-morning eastern sunlight and late-afternoon western sunlight both emit a golden glow and are tinted red, orange, pink, or variations thereof. As the day unfolds and the sun rises higher in the sky, it loses some of that warm glow. As it shines directly overhead, the sun becomes clearer, brighter, and more intense. If one of your small spaces receives hard light for an appreciable amount of the day, consider this suggestion from interior designer Patricia Gaylor, "You might want to paint the walls in a room with southern exposure in a cool color, like blue or green," she says, "to counteract the intensity of the hot sun coming in. And on northern exposures with lots of windows or skylights, paint the walls warm colors to 'heat' the spaces warm and make them cozy."

Beautiful as it can be pouring into a room, sunlight brings some other problems along with it. There's the possibility of glare and overheating, for example, and big, new windows may compromise privacy. All good reasons to assess a window-enlarging project carefully or consult a remodeling or design professional before proceeding.

Because the way sunlight flows into a room significantly affects the sense of apparent space, interior designers and architects believe that effective lighting, both natural and artificial, is even more crucial to the livability of a small space. Designer Lucianna Samu of Saratoga Springs, New York, goes even further. "It's nearly impossible," she says, "to make a small room appear larger without good-quality natural light."

It's important to keep this in mind with regard to window treatments. The less you cover the windows, the larger your small

OPPOSITE
A roof window floods a snug sewing corner with sunlight.

RIGHT
With a large east-facing window behind it, this elegant chaise makes a great spot for afternoon naps because the greatest amount of sunlight pours into the space in the morning. There is a floor lamp when extra light is needed.

room will feel. Elaborate window treatments and heavy draperies don't belong in a space that already feels cramped. If privacy or light control are issues, you may not be able to avoid window coverings completely, but try to keep them as simple as possible. Choose blinds or shades that can roll all the way up to the top of the window during the daylight hours, or hang sheers or semi-sheers. Gauzy fabrics that let the light spill in suit any type of decorating style. Lacy panels suit a country or traditional room, and plain sheers are appropriate for a contemporary-style space. If the view is so ugly that you must block it out, think about replacing the window with glass block, which will capture light but diffuse the view.

Artificial Sources

There are three major types of artificial light—general, task, and accent—and all of them can be used to enhance any modest-size room, increasing the sense of apparent space or creating coziness, or in some circumstances, both. Because you provide this light yourself, you can also fine-tune it, unlike natural light, which you have to take pretty much as it comes.

The key to devising a lighting plan that can be adjusted for different activities, the time of day, or the weather depends on understanding the different types of artificial light.

General (or ambient) *lighting* provides overall, or background, illumination and should be available in every room. Its source is often an overhead fixture, but if general lighting is well designed it does not appear to come from any one direction; instead, it surrounds the room in a general way. A good example is a wall sconce, which washes light up a wall for an overall effect. The wall reflects the light, diminishing the importance of the fixture itself. You can tell, of course, that the glow is coming from the sconce, but the overall illumination is diffused. On the other hand, a ceiling pendant that provides a bright central light with a narrow beam that can't penetrate into shadowy edges does not qualify as effective ambient light.

Recessed or semi-recessed downlights spaced across the ceiling will provide even, clear light. Depending on the type of bulb and housing used, a recessed downlight can create a wide swath of light. Semi-recessed lights, sometimes called "eyeballs," can be swiveled.

An inconspicuous quality is the key to effective ambient lighting—it is the backdrop for the room, not the main event. It changes with the environment, always providing light but never becoming obvious. For example, ambient light used in the daytime should blend with the amount of natural light entering

OPPOSITE TOP
Wall sconces, which take up no table or floor space, are handy in tight quarters, such as this bedroom.

OPPOSITE CENTER
White walls and a light floor open up this living room. Semi-sheer curtains solve the privacy problem but still admit light.

OPPOSITE BOTTOM
Bright during the day, this dining room is equipped with dimmers to alter the mood at night.

BELOW
To supplement recessed ceiling fixtures, task-light pendants hang over a kitchen food-prep counter.

through the windows. At night, you should be able to diminish the light level so that it doesn't contrast jarringly with the darkness outside.

Task lighting focuses concentrated, directional illumination over a small area for the purpose of accomplishing a specific job. The activity you want to illuminate will, in part, dictate the type of task light you choose. A desk light with an adjustable arm is ideal for paperwork. In the kitchen, under-cabinet strip fixtures give you the light you need on a work surface for chopping and dicing vegetables for a salad. A table or floor lamp lets you read a book or magazine comfortably. This type of lighting is purely functional, but it may be used in conjunction with general and accent fixtures. Although task lighting should be included in any room where specific jobs are performed, its use should be optional—you turn it on only when you need it. Don't hook up task lights to the same switch that controls a room's general illumination—using both types of light at once can create a harsh, overly bright effect.

Used to highlight an architectural feature, a painting, or another feature that's worth showing off, *accent lighting* puts the finishing touch on the room, making it come alive, creating a mood, even shaping a space. For example, cove lighting above a bathtub will delineate the bathing area dramatically; a table lamp with a wide shade will cast an attractive pool of light on a table; and a low hanging fixture will create an inviting island of light on a dining table. Without these accents a room may be well-lit, but it will lack focus and character.

A fourth category sometimes cited by specialists is *decorative lighting*. As accent lighting draws attention to an object, decorative lighting draws attention to itself. It can be kinetic, in the form of candles or flames in a fireplace, or static, in the form of a fixed wall-candelabra. Decorative lighting exists solely to attract attention. It is lighting for the sake of lighting.

Because decorative lighting is compelling, it can make you look at something—a soaring cathedral ceiling—or look away from something else: candlelight on the table in a kitchen eating area, for example, will keep people from noticing the mess of pots and pans in the sink. In this sense, decorative lighting serves a practical function as well, directing attention where you want it to go. It doesn't actually highlight anything, as accent lights do; and it doesn't provide a great deal of illumination, as ambient light does. It is the final touch in a complex, multilayered plan, a device that lighting designers love to use.

Examples of decorative light include candles, chandeliers, neon signs, strips of miniature lights—anything, in fact, that is deliberate or contrived. Include it to unify a room and strike a balance among the other types of light, including natural light from the sun and moon.

Contrast and *diffusion* are also important elements in your lighting scheme. Both task and accent lighting are examples of a high-contrast approach—they eliminate shadows and bring

smart tip

ACCENT LIGHTING

Wall-wash lighting fixtures use special trim that covers half of the aperture and directs all of the light onto the wall. These fixtures can be used to highlight large features such as fireplaces, bookcases, or paintings. They are also effective at brightening small areas, such as hallways, lightening the walls and visually extending the actual physical boundaries of the space.

objects into sharp, crisp focus. Ambient and decorative lighting are more diffused. They supply softer, more forgiving illumination and create a comfortable and relaxing atmosphere. Most rooms benefit from a combination of these two approaches, so be sure to incorporate both contrast and diffusion in your plan.

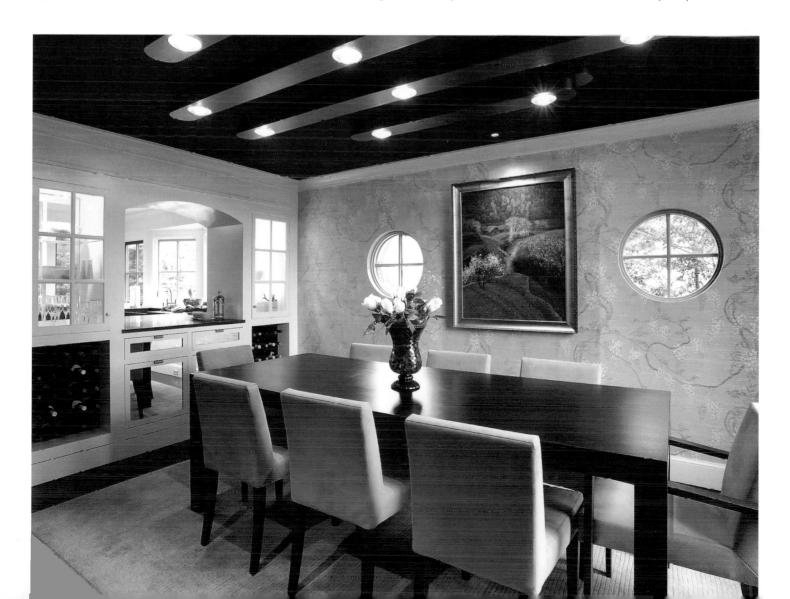

the right bulb

Just changing the types of bulbs—or "lamps," as professional lighting designers call them—in your existing household fixtures can make a major difference in the way your rooms look, function, and feel. Does this mean you should replace all of your fluorescent lamps with halogen fixtures? Well, no—this might be exaggerating the power of the right light. But don't underestimate it, either.

Understanding the differences in lamps will help you select the right light sources for all of your rooms, not just the space-challenged ones. Light is like paint. You get different effects depending on the combinations you use. And color is nothing but the reflection of different types of light. When planning a lighting scheme, always consider the relationship between color and light.

Lighting professionals assess the *color temperature* a lamp gives off—and how light from the lamp affects the objects it is lighting—by the use of scales. The term "color temperature" refers to the appearance of light in terms of the warmth or coolness of its color. Fluorescent lamps, which do not emit a continuous spectrum of light, are assigned a *correlated color temperature value* (CCT). Lamps, which range in color from red to orange to yellow to blue to blue-white, are ranked according to the Kelvin (K) temperature scale. This rating will help you select lamps that are closely matched, and you can vary coolness or warmth for specific situations. Generally, light sources below 3,000K are considered warm, while those above 4,000K are described as cool. Mid-range light sources fall between 3,200K and 3,600K.

Selecting bulbs that provide balanced lighting comfortably close to what appears normal to the eye is usually the most appealing and successful choice. In fact, most residential interiors include a combination of warm and cool tones. Experiment with various combinations to create the effect you like best, keeping in mind that balance and layering are the two keys to success. Here is a brief description of widely available bulbs and their characteristics.

Incandescent. Like sunlight, incandescent bulbs emit *continuous-spectrum light,* which contains every color. In fact, illumination from these bulbs is even warmer than sunlight, making its effect on a room very appealing. And they have a positive effect on people, too—making skin tones look good and enhancing a feeling of well-being. Drawbacks? These bulbs use a lot of electricity, produce a lot of heat, and have a short life span.

Usually made of glass (and therefore quite fragile), incandescent bulbs are available clear, diffuse, tinted, colored, or with a reflective interior coating. One type features a waterproof lens cover that makes it suitable for installing over a tub or inside a shower.

Fluorescent. New and improved, these energy-efficient bulbs cast a diffuse, shadowless light that makes them desirable for general illumination. The older fluorescents emitted an unflattering light that make skin tones look pale and bland. Newer ones, called "triphosphor fluorescent lamps," are warmer and more closely resemble sunlight. Fluorescents are available in both the familiar tube versions and in newer, compact styles.

Because the life cycle of fluorescents is shortened when they are used for periods of less than three hours, it's best to chose them for places where the light will be left on for longer than that. For example, a fluorescent might not make sense in a storage area or a powder room where the light is left on for only a few minutes at a time. But it would add up to significant energy savings used as, say, an overhead kitchen light, which would be turned on for hours at a time.

Halogen. This is actually a type of incandescent bulb that produces brighter, whiter light at a lower wattage and with greater energy efficiency. The disadvantages are a higher price tag and a higher heat output that requires a special shield for

smart tip DIMMERS

Dimmers connected to ceiling lights give you flexibility. When you want to rev up the lighting and brighten the whole room to make it look larger and more alive, you can do so. Then with a quick turn of the dial, or flick of a switch, you can dim the room down into cozy intimacy.

For economy and energy savings, you can also dim the lights just slightly to extend bulb life without making any significant change in the light level. For instance, dimming the light to 50 percent will be perceived as though you had dimmed it to only 70 percent.

fire protection. Halogen bulbs are thicker and heavier than incandescent models and have a slightly different shape. A low-voltage version, typically used for accent lighting, produces a brighter light and is even more energy efficient.

Fiber-optic systems. One of many lighting innovations gradually finding their way into the home, these systems consist of one extremely bright lamp that transports light to one or more destinations through fiber-optic cables, the same kind of cables that transmit telephone and computer signals. Currently used mostly for accent lighting, fiber-optic illumination does not generate excessive heat, making it ideal for highlighting artwork. It's also coming into use for decorative outdoor lighting and nighttime illumination for pools, spas, and hot tubs.

your lighting needs

When a room is not bright enough, many people simply exchange low-watt bulbs for high-watt ones. Wattage, however, is simply a measurement of how much electricity a lamp consumes. The actual light output of a bulb is measured in lumens. If the bulbs you're using aren't producing enough overall illumination, replace them with ones that have more lumens. The next time you shop for bulbs read the labels, which indicates the lumens per watt (lpw) produced by a bulb. The more lumens per watt, the more efficient the lamp. When looking for intensity produced by a lamp, refer to its candlepower (Cp). The more candela (units), the brighter the source.

But when planning a lighting scheme, you'll want to take other factors into consideration as well. For example, how much natural light flows into the room and how will you use it—to work or read, rest, dine, entertain, or a combination of all of these?

You'll also want to consider the reflectance levels of the room, or the amount of light that is reflected from a colored surface, such as a tile floor or a painted wall. Light colors are reflective; dark colors are absorbent. A case in point: white reflects 80 percent of the light in a room but black reflects only 4 percent of it. Surface textures are also part of the equation—mirror-like surfaces can reflect as much as 90 percent. Thus, a room with walls painted in satin or glossy white or pale colors requires less light than one painted in deep jewel tones.

Next, consider the size of the room. How high are the ceilings? High ones will require brighter lights to dispel shadows. If your ceilings are low, you may have to tone down brightness to keep light from bouncing off the ceilings and walls. How many windows are there and what directions do they face?

Most of the time, lighting designers identify requirements by using suggested foot-candle (Fc) levels for specific activities and areas. Foot-candles, which refer to the amount of light that falls on a surface, are used primarily for directional lamps. To determine the amount of foot-candle power you will need to adequately light an area, divide the candlepower of the bulb you intend to use by the distance from the fixture to the surface squared ($Fc = Cp \div D^2$).

There are no perfect formulas, but by looking at how each of these factors affects the others you can probaby devise a good lighting plan. Keeping in mind the science and technology involved in lighting will help you assess your own requirements for the room. Ideally you want to incorporate a variety of options for various activities, create a pleasant ambiance, and add a sense of spaciousness to the room. Says designer Lucianna Samu, "When I design a room, the first thing I ask myself is, 'How am I going to light this space?' Then, 'Where is the [natural] light coming from?'

"Kitchens, home offices, reading areas—all require great, not just good, lighting," says Samu. "It's not enough to stick a few recessed fixtures in a kitchen based on [desired] wattage and then call it a day," she cautions.

"To work out their lighting needs," she continues, "I would suggest that people think through a week's worth of living in any given room. Decide how it would best be lit for all its different purposes, and plan accordingly. For example, in the kitchen, first thing in the morning, before you're fully awake, it's useful to have a low, or individual, lighting scenario. People seem to understand this concept in a master suite, but it's relevant in all the other rooms of the house, too. Mixing sources—daylight, lamps, recessed fixtures, both fluorescent and incandescent bulbs—guarantees a balanced scheme that will supply the function and feeling you want the room to have."

smart steps
think ahead

Step 1 EXAMINE YOUR ACTIVITIES

Most importantly, the purpose of your lighting plan is to enhance the function of the room. If you doubt this, try preparing a complex recipe or reading the small type in an official document without the proper light. So it is logical that your first step would be to make a list of all the day and nighttime activities that may take place in the room, everything from reading, TV watching, doing homework, chatting on the phone, or working on crafts projects.

Step 2 SKETCH AN INFORMAL PLAN

Make a quick sketch of the floor plan, and circle the activity areas, such as worktables, reading chairs or sofas, TV viewing spots, and so on. Not all of the activities that will take place in the room will require the same level of light. Mark each activity area with a "G" for general illumination, "T" for task lighting, and "A" for accent lighting. In some places you will be pencil-

ing in more than one type of light—you may use an easy chair, for instance, for reading or for TV viewing or even for napping.

Locate the general illumination first; then follow that by indicating where you will need task lights; finally, decide where you want to install accent lighting. For this purpose, you might want to place some recessed fixtures over a piece of art or highlight handsome crown molding or hand-painted tile. If you like the idea of using accent lighting but don't quite know where to place it, ask yourself what is the most interesting feature in the room. It may be a wall-hung framed print, a display of treasured collectibles on a bookshelf, or a window with a beautiful view.

Step 3 CHECK THE LOCAL CODE

Every city, town, or village has codes regulating the placement of electricity near water. Before you finalize your lighting plans or invest in any fixtures—especially those intended for the kitchen or the bathroom—talk to your contractor or lighting specialist about the codes that apply in your area. If you are doing the work yourself, without any professional help, call your local building authority before you proceed.

LEFT
Cobalt pendants provide task lighting and a little bit of design pizzazz in a compact kitchen.

OPPOSITE
Careful planning created a lighting scheme that is practical in keeping with the contemporary architecture. Note the small spotlights that wash the wall behind the bed.

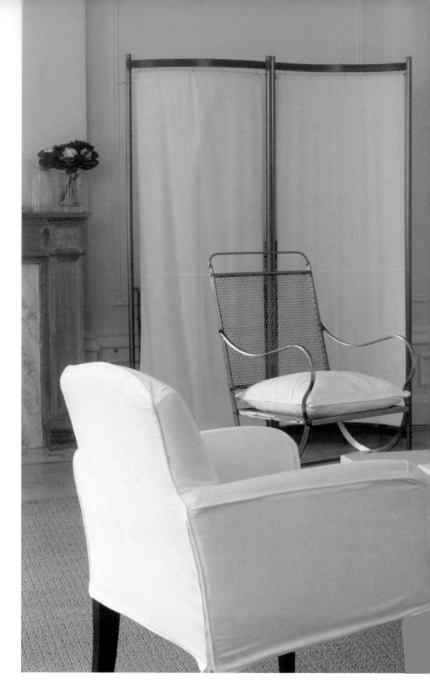

■ Step 4 SHOP THE SHOWROOMS

Here's something else to do before you proceed with your plan—visit lighting showrooms or the lighting sections of home centers and department stores. These little trips will give you the opportunity to look over the types and styles of fixtures that are available. What you see may inspire you, or at the very least help you make choices that suit your needs and the decorating sensibility of your home.

While you're there, take the time to talk to the lighting specialists that these stores often employ. Take your informal plan and list of activities with you, and if you've got fabric or flooring samples, paint chips, magazine clippings of rooms you love, or even photographs of your own rooms, stick them in your satchel, too. If you show these materials to one of the staff specialists, he or she can help you design a good plan and choose the right fixtures for implementing it. Be sure to also mention that your room is small and you want to use lighting to make it look bigger; the lighting professional will take it from there.

room by room

Lighting is practical as well as mood-altering, so don't hesitate to try out different types all over the house. First, use this room-by-room round-up to make sure you're getting the most from your current lighting scheme.

Living Areas

Living and family rooms, typically the largest spaces in the house, often don't receive enough light. Some experts suggest eliminating dark spots by placing three table or floor lamps so that they form a triangle and their halos meet or overlap when you turn on all of the fixtures at the same time. To light up all four corners of a room and eliminate deep shadows, try using tiny spotlights that sit on the floor. Unless your living room or family room is very small, avoid trying to light the whole room with a single source of overhead illumination—you don't want to draw attention to the fixture rather than to the room or the people in it. Recessed canisters are better for ambient light, and with dimming capability, you can lower the intensity to create a mood

or to eliminate glare for TV watching. Increase the feeling of space by training wall washers on light-colored ceilings and using uplights to bounce illumination off both ceilings and walls.

In both of these activity areas you may also need adequate task lighting for other activities, so be sure to take all of them into consideration.

Most lighting specialists agree that light for dining should come from an overhead fixture centered on the table. In a room with 8-foot-high ceilings, hang the fixture so that its bottom is 27 to 36 inches above the table; raise the fixture 3 inches for every additional foot of ceiling height. Chandeliers look good in a formal dining room; use shades to soften the glare of bare bulbs. A combination ceiling fan and light is suitable for an infor-

head source, which could leave a lot of the room in shadow and cause your own body to block light flowing to work areas. You might want to illuminate work zones with a pendant light, undercabinet strip lights, or recessed fixtures with controls that let you spotlight specific areas. Besides being handy, undercabinet lights can create an illusion of space.

If your kitchen is roomy enough to include an eating area—or if it opens to one—hang a pendant fixture that shines down on the table, leaving the rest of the kitchen in shadows at dinner time.

Adequate lighting is important in the kitchen for safety and function. A good lighting plan will make working in even the tiniest galley kitchen more pleasant. It might be worth it to talk to a kitchen designer, lighting specialist, or electrician about installing a new system.

smart tip

FINDING THE RIGHT MIRROR

Before you invest in expensive mirroring, make sure what you will be reflecting is what you actually want to see. Bring in a mirror you already own—as large as possible—and place it securely in a couple of spots around the room until you find an effect that you like. Check what will be reflected in the mirror by standing where it will hang and looking at the wall opposite it.

mal space. Whichever you chose, make sure the light is bright enough for close work at the dining table and can be dimmed for dining.

New York interior designer Bunny Williams takes a bit of issue with this conventional wisdom. "People's biggest mistake with this room is getting all their light from overhead sources," she says. "It's cold and not intimate." She suggests dimming overhead fixtures to mimic the look of candlelight and providing soft supplemental light with wall sconces.

If your kitchen is very small, ambient light from one or two overhead fixtures may be sufficient to brighten the whole room, make it look more spacious, and provide adequate task light at the same time. But you will probably need more than an over-

ABOVE
Decorative lighting comes in many forms, including the sensual glow of a collection of white candles.

ABOVE
Select fixtures that are in keeping with the look of the room. For example, vintage-style sconces harmonize nicely with the antique furniture and accessories in this bedroom.

OPPOSITE
Even a dazzling glass-enclosed shower will need some illumination. Ask your electrician about special fixtures that are specified for wet areas and will keep things bright—and safe.

Personal Areas

Because most bedrooms are reserved for relaxation and respite from the business of the household, subtle lighting is the goal. A small bedroom will not require a bright overhead fixture; if one exists, make sure it is shaded and can be dimmed to a soft glow. Reading lights and a lamp on a dresser or occasional table may be all the general illumination you need. But if the bedroom includes a grooming area, you will need task lighting for that as well. Clip lights that attach to the headboard or swing-arm wall lamps are good choices for reading—they focus light directly

glass block

Glass block, also often called glass brick, is an architectural material used wherever both privacy and light are desired. Architects often specify it for offices or public spaces, but it's equally useful at home, especially in small areas.

When space is at a premium and there is no room for a conventional window, consider setting a rectangle of glass block into the exterior wall. For example, in a small room that could benefit from an additional window but doesn't offer opportunities for a pleasant view, an expanse of glass block can provide the light but block the unsightliness. Retrofitted with glass block, an existing window that overlooks an ugly view becomes a thing of beauty—and light.

In the bath, an expanse of glass block can take the place of a traditional window—or even cover most of an exterior wall—providing privacy without blocking the light flow. It can also be used as a privacy wall or in place of plate glass as a shower enclosure. To light up an undersized foyer or narrow entrance hallway, consider flanking the front door with sidelights composed of glass block. You can also use this versatile material as an interior wall or partition, replacing part of a solid wall or defining separate areas. Utilized in this way, a section of glass block extends interior sight lines and maximizes available light, both key strategies for making small spaces look bigger.

Glass block is available in a variety of finishes, some of which offer more privacy than others. Some are virtually see-through; others admit light but distort forms so that they are almost unrecognizable; still others admit 100 percent of available light but completely obstruct views. Major manufacturers make it easy to spruce up your house with glass block, offering such handy items as pre-assembled partition walls and glass-block shower kits. Preassembled glass-block windows in vinyl-clad wood frames are also readily available. Assembled at the factory, these units are shipped ready to install and go up as easily as a traditional pane-glass window.

onto your pages and away from your sleeping partner.

Children's rooms need a little more brightness. Generous overall illumination from an overhead fixture should be combined with effective task lights at the bedside and the desk. Some kids also need a night light. Avoid floor lamps—they're too easy to knock onto the floor.

A bathroom that measures less than 100 square feet only needs one light fixture, say the experts; for every additional 50 square feet, add another one. This is a good general rule, but assess your own bathroom to be sure you have enough warm-toned overall illumination to reach into every corner. Dark corners compromise safety in a room that inherently poses hazards.

No matter how small the bathroom is, you should augment any overhead fixture with task lighting in the vanity area. Why cheat yourself of the illumination you need for shaving, brushing your teeth, and applying makeup? Task lighting at the mirror should come at you from both sides, radiating from the middle of your face. Lighting that comes from above creates harsh, unflattering shadows.

You might also consider adding a light to the shower or tub area. Consult a professional to make sure you get a fixture that is expressly designed for use in wet areas.

light tricks

Lighting experts tell us that mirrors and other reflective surfaces can reflect as much as 90 percent of the light in a room, which translates into a lot of extra brightness. The brightness then translates into an illusion of spaciousness because the more light there is in a room, the larger it usually feels. Take advantage of the light-reflecting quality of mirrors by using larger ones in bathrooms, powder rooms, or bedrooms, and also by introducing them in unexpected places, such as kitchens and family rooms, to add life to dark areas and to banish peripheral shadows. Any small space feels smaller if it has dark corners.

Consider also such shiny surfaces as glass-topped tables, highly reflective furniture finishes, glass doors in place of solid ones, and glossy or lacquered paints for walls or furniture. Harnessing the powers of reflection to enhance the feeling of space can result in a glitzy decor, more over-the-top than may suit your sensibilities, but not necessarily. There are also tasteful, low-key ways to use this strategy.

Take mirrors, for instance. This decorating tool can fool the eye into seeing a space as larger than it actually is, but it also calls for restraint. You must make sure, the experts warn, that the mirrors you hang reflect a view that you actually want to see. Also, make sure that mirrors do not create an unpleasant glare in the room. Interior designer Lynette Jennings puts it this way, "Mirrors expand space only when they reflect a spatial element." You can double a view, she says, by hanging a mirror opposite a window—but be sure you're doubling something pleasant and not a panorama of a rickety shed and a driveway full of cars. Similarly, a mirror may look fabulous hanging over a fireplace, but what is it reflecting? You don't want to see the reflection of a blank wall or the image of tabletops at an awkward angle. On the other hand, hanging the mirror on that blank wall would reflect the fireplace and mantel, a better idea.

Jennings has other tips. "Reflect an adjacent wall to visually lengthen a room, or create an image of infinity by reflecting a corner where two walls come together." It's important to remember, says this designer, that "mirrors double everything."

Los Angeles stylist and designer Sunday Hendrickson is not a big fan of using a mirror as a space-extender. "Many people advise using them," she says, "but I think it's the worst thing you can do—it just reflects all the business." Mirroring the kitchen backsplash is often suggested as a space stretcher for a tiny kitchen. In some circumstances it can be effective and also add a lovely sparkle. But to make it work you must keep what it reflects—your countertops—pristinely neat. Otherwise these little strips of mirror will just reflect clutter and magnify it, providing unsightly proof of Lynette Jennings's claim that mirrors double everything. In addition, you have to clean food splatters.

LEFT
In a kitchen, under-cabinet lights brighten the work surface—an important safety feature when you're working with sharp knives.

OPPOSITE
A strip of small, under-counter lights, covered with glare-free frosted glass, is a creative way to add decorative light. The small pendant focuses task light on the work surface.

LEFT
Illuminated geometric shapes in the ceiling create overall brightness and add architectural drama to this room at the same time. Another dramatic effect was added by the sculptural pendants over the dining table.

Even if you veto the idea of mirrored backsplashes, mirror and glass can be effective space-stretchers elsewhere in the kitchen. Clear- or frosted-glass doors on wall cabinets create openness instead of stopping the eye at a solid door; mirrored cabinet doors would also open things up, as would lining a cabinet with mirror to display your best crystal or china. If any doors lead from your kitchen to the outside, to another living space, or to a mudroom, extend sightlines by removing the doors completely or replacing them with a glass unit. If the mudroom is not always neat, hang a filmy curtain on the glass door; you'll camouflage the mess but still gain light and openness.

Letting these cautions be your guide, there is almost no limit to the places you can effectively add mirror. In the bath, a large mirror or even an entirely mirrored wall opens up space amazingly. In a tiny windowless bath, hanging a mirror works almost as well as adding a window. Be sure to position the mirror no lower than waist high, though, so that it doesn't reflect anything unsightly, such as plumbing lines or toilets. A small bath also benefits from the use of glass and other shiny surfaces—a clear glass shower door extends your sightline. Consider a glass countertop for the vanity for additional reflection.

In the living room, a mirror that reflects a garden view, a painting, or an attractive architectural feature is a good space expander, as is a mirror that stretches sightlines by providing a view into an adjoining area. If it suits the style of your room, you might also place an extra-large mirror on one wall, then hang a smaller one on the wall opposite it. This trick creates the illusion of infinite space. To add depth to a bookcase, mirror the backs of the shelves.

Dining rooms are wonderful places for mirrors, says

smart tip SKYLIGHTS

Skylights and roof windows can capture daylight and create the illusion of space in all parts of the house, which is a blessing for any small room. But during the summer months, they can also make a room uncomfortably hot. To avoid overheating, don't orient skylights or roof windows toward the south or west unless, as in the case of a roof window, they can be opened or effectively shaded during the afternoon heat. An open south-facing roof window can actually help cool a room because the hot air will rise up and flow outside.

Another tip: a skylight that is located at the edge of a room is more effective at maximizing visual space because incoming light is reflected off the walls.

Lynette Jennings, "because they are essentially a stage with four background walls." Mirrored tabletops can also be effective in a dining room, but make sure they do not pick up a strong glare from recessed lighting or chandelier bulbs. Little chandelier shades or a fixture that uses candles instead of lightbulbs can solve the glare problem.

In the bedroom, use a mirror to reflect the outdoors if you can. Another idea is to affix mirrors to the front of closet doors. Covering the entire door, top to bottom, edge to edge would be a nice touch in a contemporary room. In a more traditional space, you could install the mirror in the recessed panels of the doors so that it looks framed.

Furniture can also be mirrored. A round table with a mirrored top can add openness and glamour to a bedroom. A small chest of drawers or tables can be completely mirrored, as well. However, too much mirror would give a room a garish and chaotic look, but a reflective piece of furniture here and there can be quite effective. A mirrored folding screen can transform a dreary corner into a light and airy space.

A glass-topped or mirrored dining table will work wonders in a small room, and the transparency of small-scale, glass-topped pieces such as coffee tables or end tables helps expand the amount of visible space.

In any room, glass tables—large or small—take up very little visual space and, in fact, they almost seem to disappear. It's always important to choose shatter-proof glass, however. That is particularly important in a home with young children. As an alternative, you could choose a clear plastic table. These look especially slick in a modern interior or one with a 1970s retro sensibility. You might consider pairing one with traditional furnishings for an interesting eclectic look.

A more subtle trick is to use shiny finishes on furniture, cabinets, even on the walls. Like mirrors, shiny surfaces reflect available light. In the kitchen, for example, you could select cabinets with a metallic or a glossy laminate surface. Glass countertop tiles or polished stone would also add sparkle and expansiveness. Lacquered, shiny furniture is available for all of your other rooms, too, in the form of dining tables, coffee tables, occasional pieces, headboards, desks, and bath cabinets.

Glossy and lacquered paints can also bring a room-altering shimmer to your rooms. Because their light-reflecting quality makes walls recede even more than ordinary light-colored walls do, these paints give you an extra edge. But before you apply a paint with a high sheen, check the condition of your walls. To get the best results, they should be smooth and free of serious imperfections. When in doubt, talk to a knowledgeable salesperson at your local paint store or home center.

smart tip CATCH THE LIGHT

In the living room, small torchères placed on the floor behind a sofa or an armchair will wash light up the walls, adding the illusion of height. This little lighting trick is especially effective if the walls are painted a light color.

LEFT
Dimmed lighting and strategically placed downlights soften the rectilinear lines in this open loft space.

OPPOSITE
In an all-white bathroom with a wall-to-wall mirror and other reflective surfaces a little light goes a long way.

design workbook
LIGHT-DEFINED SPACE

on the level

In a one-room apartment, lighting and changes in levels define living areas. Strip lights accentuate a wooden bench that runs along the wall and highlight stairs to the elevated sleeping area. An elongated skylight illuminates almost the entire length of the space. Well-placed recessed canister lights supply general illumination.

on the window

In the living area, top left, a translucent, floor-to-ceiling shade cuts glare from the window, allowing daytime TV viewing.

on the surface

Frosted-glass doors, stainless steel, and under-cabinet strips brighten the kitchen, far left.

in the bath

All-white and glass surfaces visually expand the tiny bathroom, left.

design workbook
A COMPACT VACATION HOUSE

here comes the sun

A double-height wall of glass spills light into every corner of a vacation house in the woods. Deep eaves and the year-round foliage of ever-green trees protect the rooms from hot summer sun. In winter, the stone floor acts as a heat sink, collecting the sun's heat and releasing it at night.

on the light side

Light-color pine lines the walls, top left. The focal point of the living area is a stone fireplace with a stucco chimney. A Native American wall hanging adds a touch of color.

a bright beacon

At night, the lighted house looks inviting from outside, top right.

a thoughtful detail

Small lights along the stair wall are an important safety feature, left.

design workbook
URBANE PLAN

true enlightenment

A professionally designed lighting plan creates the quiet mood in this minimalist yet sophisticated master bedroom.

uplifting downlights

Small lights are partially hidden but cast a glow onto the ledge behind the bed. (See also top left and right.)

upon reflection

Light, warm tones used throughout on both hard and soft surfaces enhance the restful effect.

moody accent

When viewed from outside the room, left, the soft downlighting looks decorative, making the wall above the bed appear to glow.

light support

Dark floors throughout, left, appear to recede, enhancing the the light show.

design workbook

A WORLD OF WINDOWS

on top of the world

Part of a West Coast duplex apartment, this sunspace provides light-filled interiors, panoramic views, and access to an outdoor roof-top living area.

cozy corner

The duplex's open-plan lower level, also fitted with large expanses of glass, contains a compact kitchen and a living and dining area, top left. At night, the owners dim the recessed ceiling fixtures and enjoy the sparkle of the city lights. The windows all have shades to control sun glare and heat buildup on hot days.

a space in the sun

Tucked into a sunny corner, the kitchen cleanup area, left, enjoys more of the view.

LEFT
Undaunted by the
lack of a yard, city
dwellers created a
rooftop oasis, with
potted plants, a
small dining area,
and ornament.

9

outdoor areas

THE GREAT ESCAPE   FURNISHING YOUR OUTDOOR OASIS   SUNSPACES
CONTAINER GARDENS   OUTDOOR LIGHTING   DESIGN WORKBOOK

Extending your living spaces to the outdoors can make a small home live larger. So step outside and investigate your options. But it may be possible that the outside of your house is as space-challenged as the inside. Don't let a small lot or a postage-stamp-size backyard stop you from enjoying some alfresco living. Limited space notwithstanding, there are several things you can do—attach a deck to your house, place a patio in the yard's most scenic spot, revive a tired front porch, or even add a sunspace to enhance the actual or perceived size of your house. If you live in an apartment or condominium, you may not have a yard you can call your own, but don't give up on outdoor living—instead, check out the possibilities that may exist on your balcony or even up on the roof. The ideas in this chapter will get you started.

BELOW
A ground-level deck increases usable living space for a suburban house and gives the indoor rooms something pretty to see.

OPPOSITE
Located just outside the master bedroom, a raised deck offers treetop views and a private spot for soaking up the sun.

the great escape

Alfresco living areas connect indoors and out and extend usable space during pleasant weather, which can make a small house feel less cramped and confining. And just as a window to the garden seems to visually stretch the boundaries of interior walls, a glass door—or a set of sliding glass doors—that leads outside elongates sightlines and creates a new sense of interior spaciousness.

Decks

Adding a deck is a popular project. It's generally easy, so many do-it-yourself homeowners can handle it. It's economical—in fact, a deck addition is one the most reasonably priced home improvement projects you can undertake. It's worthwhile—the finished product offers a wealth of outdoor living possibilities. And here's a bonus—adding a deck will increase the resale value of your home for less than what it would cost to add a front porch or build an addition.

Ground-level decks, suitable for flat locations, resemble low platforms. They may extend living space by adjoining a house or sit freestanding wherever you want to put them. If your yard is very small, it's probably best to attach a deck directly to the house.

Sometimes the slope of a yard or the design of a house makes anything but a raised deck impractical. If your house has a walkout basement, a raised deck will easily extend the living space of a kitchen, living room, or family room. And one flight up, a raised deck enhances the livability of a second-story bedroom. If

your site is large enough, you might consider a multilevel deck, with the levels connected by stairs or ramps. Sets of stairs that connect one level to another provide a division between lounging, cooking, and eating areas. This type of deck often devotes one level to a spa or a hot tub.

Traditionally, decks have been built from wood—redwood; pressure-treated pine; cedar; or tropical hardwoods. Thanks to some recent technological developments, there are two new categories of decking—extruded vinyl and composite, which is made from natural fibers and recycled plastic. These engineered products are initially more expensive than wood, but they offer significant savings over time because they require almost no maintenance.

Wood decks look better longer if they receive some protection from the elements. A water-repellent finish will keep the wood from shrinking or splintering, and a wood preservative will slow down deterioration and decay. Many people also apply paint or stain to a deck. Semitransparent stains let the wood grain show through it. Opaque stains and paint conceal the grain of the wood and cover up its flaws. The use of a semi-transparent stain will make the wood stand out against the house. If you're after a unified look, use an opaque stain or paint that will replicate the paint color of your house.

Plan the size of your deck to accommodate the activities that will take place there. If you intend to use it for relaxing, cooking, eating, and entertaining, you'll need to allow plenty of space and sturdy underpinnings to support furniture, equipment, and people. And factor in the extra weight should you want to outfit your deck with a hot tub or major cooking appliances or even a fully equipped outdoor kitchen. The latter might feature granite countertops, a built-in cooktop and grill, a full-size sink, built-in storage cabinets, and an eating bar.

If outdoor space is limited or budget constrictions apply, don't overlook the value of a small deck, which can still be very useful, extending living space outdoors and providing an open-air extension to a kitchen, family room, or bedroom. Even a tiny deck can hold a couple of chairs, a small table, and a no-frills grill or hibachi. To maximize usefulness, consider building in a couple of space-saving benches and a table; add a few planters and fill them with flowers, and you've got an outdoor oasis.

If you decide to build the deck yourself, you'll find easy-to-follow plans at your local home center, on the Internet, or in plans books and magazines. You can also turn the project over to a professional. An architect, remodeling contractor, or a landscape architect may provide design ideas as well as installation.

Some landscaping contractors also design and install decks; or you can hire a local carpenter to build the deck from the plans you have selected.

RIGHT
Topped with a pergola and dotted with potted plants, this slate patio makes an elegant little dining pavilion. Glass doors expand interior sightlines, extending the house's small interior spaces.

select a site

Before you start construction on your outdoor living space, study the site carefully.

- Will prevailing winds make it too breezy?
- Will it be too sunny or shady?
- Does it overlook pleasant views? If not, consider another site or add plantings that will be pretty to view.
- Does it offer privacy? If not, will a section of lattice or some shrubbery help?

Porches provide their own shade, but decks and patios may need a little help for at least part of the day. Here are some options:

- Permanent coverings include pergolas or latticework roofs, which provide dappled sunshine but no protection from rain. Solid roofs of shingle, metal, or plastic panels offer total shade and keep the rain off but will add to the cost. Whichever option you choose, integrate it with the style and materials of your house for a visually pleasing look.
- Fabric coverings include various sizes of awnings, some of which are retractable; shade tents, which consist of fabric stretched over a lightweight movable frame; and umbrellas, which come in a variety of sizes and stylish shapes and in a wide selection of bright colors and cheerful patterns.

Patios and Terraces

Unlike decks, most of which are attached directly to a house, patios and terraces can be located anywhere in your yard—adjoining the house, in a scenic part of the garden, or right next to a little pond or swimming pool. A well-designed patio, no matter how small it is, will quickly become a second living room.

If you've seen some unimaginative patios, you may think of them as boring slabs of concrete. But paving has come a long way lately, and there are many attractive materials from which to choose. Any of these materials—or a creative mix of them—can produce a handsome outdoor spot.

Brick is an elegant and time-honored choice, but stone patio pavers, generally more durable than brick, can also look great. Your choices include granite, sandstone, slate, quartzite, marble, or limestone. Concrete pavers, an economical alternative to natural stone, come in a wide variety of sizes. Thanks to new methods of stamping the concrete, patterns and textures that resemble real stone are also available. Another economical choice is a composite material that closely resembles stone. Available in a range of earthy colors, such as grays, beiges, and rusts, some with green or blue highlights, these composites are usually carried by home centers.

Before you select a material for your patio or terrace, try to get a look at a good-size piece of it, or even better, ask to see it used in a finished patio. Catalog or magazine photos don't always present an accurate picture. And to complete your patio homework, ask your landscape architect, contractor, or home center which patio materials stand up best to weather conditions in your area.

A patio can be as simple or elaborate as you choose. Before you decide, think about how you will use it. What about seating? Will you want both reclining and upright chairs? Will you need both dining and occasional tables? If you'll be cooking on the patio, factor in the size of a portable grill or a built-in appliance. If you live in an urban area or on a busy suburban street, a water feature is a smart amenity—the sound of moving water can camouflage ambient noise.

Patios, like decks, make satisfying do-it-yourself projects for skilled amateurs. Some materials can be set in sand; others may have to be set in concrete. But to avoid ending up with that boring slab of concrete, get some design ideas from books, magazines, or the Internet. If your dream patio is elaborate, you can turn the job over to a landscape architect or hire a garden designer to do the creative work and a landscape contractor for the installation.

Porches

Time-honored places to relax, read a book, and watch the world go by, front porches are ideal for stretching living space and providing an open-air sitting room. A necessity before air-conditioning, porches fell from favor after World War II, but they are coming back in some areas and they grace the facades of many new houses. In fact, according to the National Association of Home Builders (NAHB), more than 50 percent of new homes are now built with front porches of some kind. In 2003, the Committee on Urban Environment in Minneapolis, Minnesota, had this to say about it: "The unique transitional space of a front porch adds value and livability to existing homes, character to the streetscape, and makes neighborhoods safer by placing more eyes on the street."

If you're lucky, you house already possesses a front porch that can be spiffed up and pressed into service as a light and airy supplemental living space. If the porch is in fairly good shape you can easily revitalize it with a thorough cleaning, some minor repair to railings and balusters, and a couple of coats of paint. If you want more privacy than the typical porch offers, you might hang some bamboo shades that roll down whenever you feel too exposed.

If your existing porch is sagging and slumping, it'll need to be shored up, reattached, and slightly slanted away from the main house so that rainwater drains off. Unless you are very skilled, these are not do-it-yourself jobs. Instead, call a reliable local remodeling contractor or carpenter.

Adding a new porch or completely replacing a decrepit one will require a larger investment of time and money than a deck or patio, but you may find it a worthwhile project. It will give you an extra room for many months of the year, provide hours of pleasurable relaxation, add architectural distinction to your house, and increase the house's value at resale time.

RIGHT
In the summer-time, what's better than relaxing on an old-fashioned covered porch with a book and a cool drink? Furnished for comfort with a settee, a couple of chairs, a pile of pillows, and a foot rest, it's a perfect outdoor living room from morning until night.

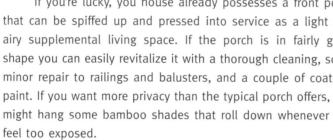

smart tip DOUBLE-DUTY FURNITURE

To furnish a small outdoor space, look for versatile, multipurpose pieces. One such piece, a resin chair, easily converts to a chaise longue. All you do is slide out an attachment that's stored under the seat. An ottoman can do triple duty—as a footrest, a seat, or a small table. Benches with lidded seats provide storage for cushions, tableware, charcoal for the grill, or gardening tools.

furnishing your outdoor oasis

A roomy front porch on a traditional house cries out for wicker or wood furniture, a pair of rockers, even an old-fashioned glider or porch swing. Depending on how you use the porch, you might also add a small dining table and chairs. A table lamp or two will add coziness, brighten a rainy afternoon, illuminate your summer reading, and extend the usability of the porch well into evening.

Decks and patios, no matter how small, can also be furnished for comfort. There is a huge amount of outdoor furniture available for every budget, ranging from plastic, wood, and glass to wrought iron and other metals. With so many choices available, you'll have no problem creating an outdoor oasis with comfortable seating, a couple of side tables, and a dining table and chairs. If you don't want to invest heavily in new pieces, scour flea markets and garage sales for chairs or tables you can paint

or varnish for new life in the great outdoors. Another cost-cutting strategy—cover your own cushions with weatherproof fabric.

Because the demarcation between indoor and outdoor spaces is becoming less and less definite, many designers now suggest that homeowners create a seamless visual flow between the two. Use furniture, accessories, and colors that harmonize with what you've got inside, they say, although they do allow that you can get away with brighter and bolder colors outdoors.

If you want to evoke the feeling of an outdoor living room, add patterned cushions, decorative planters filled with fragrant blooms, a weatherproof rug that resists fading and mildew, and favorite objects from your house or garden—a wrought-iron plant stand, a pretty table lamp, a stone sculpture, or a mercury ball, to name just a few possibilities. Make it scenic at night, too, with candles, hurricane lamps, and tiny lights strung into the branches of nearby trees. Outdoor heaters and cooling devices now help to extend the outdoor season, too.

Whether you follow this design advice or not, furnish your outdoor rooms in a style that harmonizes with the architectural character of your house. A cozy cottage scheme would look ludicrous on a deck outside of a streamlined contemporary house; conversely, sleek, hard-edged glass and metal furniture is too modern for a romantic Victorian front porch.

LEFT
A simple ground-level deck that's dedicated to outdoor dining adjoins the house and captures scenic water views and balmy breezes.

OPPOSITE
Proving that decks can be elaborate, too, this version features a roof, ceiling fans, long curtains, and an eclectic collection of furniture.

sunspaces

Often referred to as Indoor-outdoor rooms, sunspaces can give you some extra square footage in a hurry and connect you to the outdoors in any weather. Hugely popular during the oil-crisis years of the 1970s, when they were touted for their ability to provide passive-solar heating, sunspaces have stayed popular, although many people do not use them to provide winter heat.

Constructed of wood or metal frames that hold large expanses of glass in place, sunspaces can be added to your house quickly, quicker in fact than a standard wood-frame addition. Prices vary greatly but some small models—say, 7 feet long by 10 feet deep—sell for about $10,000, not including foundation work and installation. Designs vary from the nostalgic look of an English greenhouse to sleek ultra-modern models with many styles and sizes in between.

You can use a sunspace to expand any of your rooms – kitchen, living room, or bedroom—or to stand alone as a sunny sitting area and a place for plants to thrive. Many people use them as spas, with a hot tub and lots of plants drinking in the sun and moisture. One of these sunny enclosures will do more than expand your living space—it will also expand your interior horizons, making any room it adjoins feel larger and more open. And if you position the sunspace to efficiently catch low-angle winter sun, it can reduce your energy bills by up to 30 percent.

But consider carefully before you commit yourself. A sunspace must be carefully sited for overall comfort and effectiveness. Due-south is the best orientation, but 30 degrees east or west of due south is also acceptable, according to experts. A north-facing structure will not be warm enough, and a westerly direction will harness too much heat, making the addition unusable for much of the day.

Although the sunspace concept is simple, siting one correctly, and choosing the appropriate type of glazing, insulation, and window coverings is a bit complex. Be sure you buy your unit from a reliable company that has been in business for at least 10 years. If you choose a kit system, you may get some design help from the manufacturer. If not, consult a specialist before you proceed. The angle of the sun, types of glazing, and choice of flooring materials should be reviewed by an expert.

ABOVE
What a way to start the day! With the garden in full bloom, breakfast on the terrace is like being on a vacation at home.

OPPOSITE
An indoor room with an outdoor feeling, this rustic sunspace supplies bucolic views in all directions.

smart tip OUTDOOR KITCHENS

If you've got the space outdoors, you might want to go beyond burgers on the barbie and invest in a fully loaded outdoor kitchen. And it will be an investment. A top-drawer version of this latest outdoor-living luxury, which includes equipment for food-prep, cooking, cooling, and cleanup, could set you back $15,000 or more.

It's pricey, yes, but an outdoor cooking area that qualifies as a second kitchen will increase the resale value of your home, especially if you live in a temperate climate that allows you to cook out most of the year. Fortunately, less-expensive modular cabinet and bar systems are widely available as well.

Before you buy, there are a couple of things to consider. First, do you have enough deck or patio space for the food-prep equipment (36 inches on either side of the grill, experts advise), a dining table and chairs, and aisles that let people move about easily? Second, can you provide utility hookups? Your outdoor kitchen will need access to electrical, plumbing and possibly gas lines; and you can save time and money by arranging for these hookups in the early stages of the project. Third, is there enough light? Extend the hours that your outdoor kitchen Is usable buy providing an appropriate lighting plan. You will want most of the illumination to be soft and natural, but the cooking area proper, stairs, and pathways should receive brighter light.

container gardens

No space outdoors for a garden? Not to worry. Even if your yard is miniscule—or nonexistent—and your deck or patio less than generous, you can create a lush garden in containers, especially if you vary colors, shapes, and sizes for an eye-catching mix of bloom and greenery. Properly tended, most plants will thrive anywhere, even on a sunny balcony or a rooftop. Here's more good news: just about anything that can be grown in a flower bed can be grown in a container, even vegetables. And these mini-gardens are portable—you can move your containers around to create special effects, add or subtract plants at will, and give them all the ideal mix of sun and shade.

And there's good news when it comes to containers, too—anything goes. Use standard pots, which are available in a wealth of materials, sizes, shapes, and colors, or converted bowls, buckets, boxes, barrels, or whatever takes your fancy, into a planter. You can also find planters that complement the design and architecture of your deck, patio, porch, or balcony—and your house. Or build some from your decking material.

Hanging baskets are also a good choice, and built-in planters will save floor space. Just be sure that you choose rot-resistant woods such as redwood or cedar and follow the cardinal rule of containers: provide drainage. Without drainage holes, a lushly planted container will soon become a rotting, soggy mess. A word to the wise: avoid ugly water stains on the wood by putting your containers on saucers—and, if possible, elevating them—not directly on the surface of the deck.

Before buying plants, observe your site for a couple of days, assessing the amount of light and shade it receives. Then purchase plants with requirements that meet your conditions. In gardener lingo "full sun" means direct sunlight all day during the

gazebos

In great demand a few decades ago when Victorian design was the rage, garden gazebos are still popular and could be just the ticket for a backyard that doesn't lend itself to a patio or deck. These little roofed shelters, typically open on all sides to catch breezes, can be used for dining, entertaining, or just plain relaxing; and large ones can also hold a spa or hot tub.

Gazebos run the gamut from expensive cedar pavilions to more economical treated-lumber or vinyl models, and the designs range from ornate—as befits an artifact from the Victorian era—to simple. Sizes and features vary greatly, too. Most manufacturers offer a long list of options. You can design your own gazebo and build it from scratch or buy an assemble-yourself kit that you, the manufacturer's crew, or your remodeling contractor can put up in record time.

In some areas it may be necessary to obtain a building permit, especially if your proposed gazebo is a permanent structure that includes electricity or plumbing.

summer; "light shade" means four to six hours of sun daily or a pattern of shade all day; "partial shade" translates to two to four hours of sun daily or dappled shade all day; in "full shade" there's no direct sun, only reflected light. Does your outdoor space have a lot of shady moments during the day? No problem. There are plenty of plants that thrive in shade, and even those plants that love the sun may benefit from afternoon shade, especially on hot summer days.

Ask your local nursery about plants that will do well in your area, which ones will thrive in your specific growing conditions, and what type of potting mixes are best for the plants you want. Although you can grow some plants in an all-purpose planting mix, others need special formulas for success.

LEFT
With no backyard space, this little house confines its horticultural activity to an entry garden, complete with containers and window boxes overflowing with plants and flowers in bloom.

OPPOSITE AND BELOW
In the middle of New York City, a backyard garden blossoms with color. Containers hold everything from flowers to shrubs to small trees. Lush ivy climbs up the latticework. Furniture includes a table and chairs, a potting cart, and a market umbrella for shade, especially when transplanting.

outdoor lighting

If you have taken the time, trouble, and expense to create an outdoor area that extends your interior living spaces, wouldn't it be a shame to use it only during daylight hours? With proper artificial lighting, you can hang out half the night if you want. A comprehensive outdoor lighting plan will include task lights, overall illumination for safety and security, and accent and decorative lights for nighttime drama and ambiance, of course!

smart steps
light it right

Step 1 SUPPLY TASK LIGHTING

What good is a cozy deck or a picturesque patio if you can't see what you're doing once the sun goes down?

Your local lighting showroom or home center carries a wealth of fixtures that can shed light on your nighttime alfresco activities, but first decide how much light you actually need and where it should go. You will probably want to locate fixtures near food preparation, cooking, and wet-bar zones. You'll also want to illuminate the areas designated for drinks, snacks, and buffets. Be sure, too, that there is adequate light near dining tables, conversation areas, and recreational spots such as the hot tub, if you plan to use it in the evening. If your outdoor area will include a complete kitchen, you will also need outlets for a refrigerator, small appliances, and freestanding fixtures such as lamps and heating devices.

Because you won't always be using all of these areas at one time—and some require brighter light than others—separate switches, each one with a dimmer, will be helpful.

Remember, at night, a little light goes a long way. Bright, intense lighting can look harsh and unpleasant and is not necessary for most of the outside activities listed above. Subtle illumination is a better choice. Even light bright enough to read by can be restricted to a single fixture that doesn't impinge on the overall scheme.

Step 2 ADD ACCENTS

Accent lighting, also referred to as "architectural lighting," is strictly decorative. While accent lighting may illuminate a dim stairway or a dark path, its main purpose is not to provide safety or security but to create a play of light and shadow that dramatizes the exterior of your house after dark. In Chapter Seven you learned about using accent lighting indoors to highlight a painting or a handsome design detail—imagine how effective the same technique can be outdoors as it plays up an appealing architectural or garden feature or just bathes your yard in soft and subtle light.

Uplighting, for example, can give trees, shrubs, or garden structures such as gazebos or arbors a dramatic night life. And, effectively lit, trees and shrubs will look just as good after their leaves have fallen and the branches are bare. Accent lighting can also cast a glow on a pond, fountain, or a pretty flower bed, creating nighttime drama that's visible from your deck, patio, or porch.

There are dozens of types of low-voltage accent fixtures—tulip lamps, ivy lights, miniature lanterns, strips to outline a curving path, soft downlights in the branches of a tree to simulate the moonlight, and wall washers to create special effects on a partition or against the house.

Although you can easily install low-voltage accent lighting yourself, it takes some thought to get it right. You might want to hire a lighting designer or landscape architect to get you started or read some of the excellent guides available. The words "low-voltage exterior lighting" will lead you to helpful guides on the Internet or at your local library or bookstore.

Step 3 ENSURE SAFETY

It's not enough to illuminate tasks and highlight appealing features. To ensure the safety of neighbors, friends, and family,

your overall plan should also shed light on outdoor walkways, paths, stairs, transition areas—say, from the deck to the yard, hot tub, or pool—or any area where you routinely walk outside the house. Be sure to also adequately light the driveway and all entrances to the house, including any doorways that lead to outdoor areas, particularly if you must step up or down to reach them.

Your safety lighting does not have to be ultra-bright; it is enough if it allows you to clearly see where you are going after dark. Resist the impulse to over-light. Many homeowners make the mistake of installing too many lights, especially along walkways and driveways. Over-lighting these areas creates an ugly, airport run-way sort of look. Low-voltage lights installed in posts, in stair risers, or along walkways are adequate to light your way safely in most cases.

To avoid bumps and bruises, the edges of built-in planters or benches and any other sharp corners should also be delineated with small lights.

deck design software

Programs you can run on your home computer can help you organize your design ideas. Produced by a number of companies, the software makes simple work of drawing decks, railings, planters, and other outdoor-living ameni-ties. Some versions show your work in three-dimensional rotating images that allow you to take a virtual tour of the deck and the surrounding area. Some of the programs also provide materials lists and building instructions.

BELOW LEFT
Vintage-style lanterns are a nice touch on the flower-bedecked front gate of this traditional house; stone columns and a pergola give the entry serious architectural presence.

BELOW
Hanging lamps gently illuminate a rugged southwestern-style back porch.

design workbook
TREEHOUSE GETAWAY

an airy aerie

Perched in the branches of a venerable old tree, this little house offers a place to retreat without leaving home. On the deck, there's seating and a few potted blooms.

easygoing elegance

In the creamy-white interior, the comforts of home beckon—books, photos, collect-ibles, and a comfy wicker rocking chair, top left.

tea for two

Like something out of a fairy tale, a little table and chairs make a sweet setting for tea, far left

decorative details

Throughout, the space between the studs is devoted to shelves for favorite objects, bottom left.

pièce de résistance

An old sofa has been outfitted for afternoon snoozes, middle left.

appendix TEMPLATES

Sofas, Love Seats, and Sofa Beds

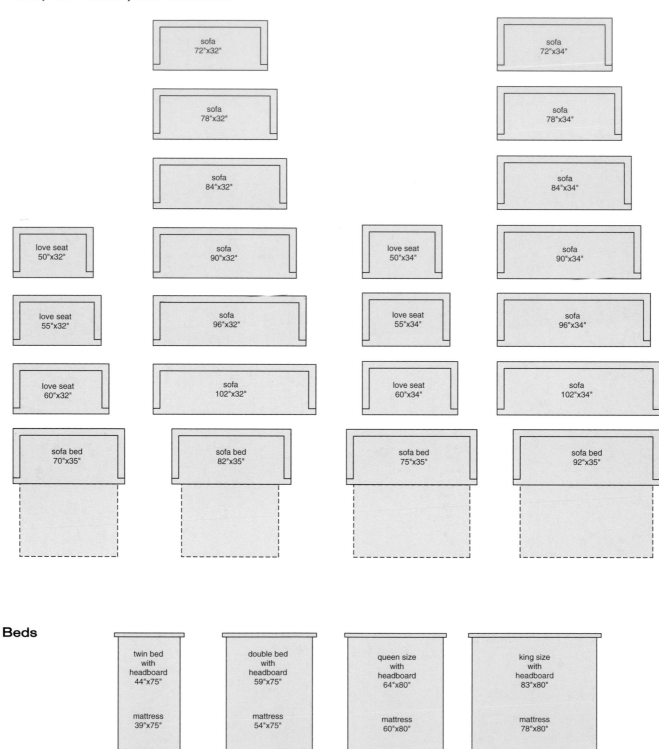

sofa
72"x32"

sofa
72"x34"

sofa
78"x32"

sofa
78"x34"

sofa
84"x32"

sofa
84"x34"

love seat
50"x32"

sofa
90"x32"

love seat
50"x34"

sofa
90"x34"

love seat
55"x32"

sofa
96"x32"

love seat
55"x34"

sofa
96"x34"

love seat
60"x32"

sofa
102"x32"

love seat
60"x34"

sofa
102"x34"

sofa bed
70"x35"

sofa bed
82"x35"

sofa bed
75"x35"

sofa bed
92"x35"

Beds

twin bed
with
headboard
44"x75"

mattress
39"x75"

double bed
with
headboard
59"x75"

mattress
54"x75"

queen size
with
headboard
64"x80"

mattress
60"x80"

king size
with
headboard
83"x80"

mattress
78"x80"

Chairs and Ottomans

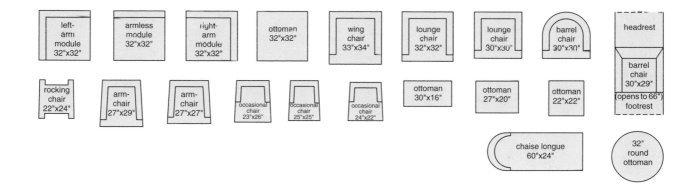

left-arm module 32"x32" armless module 32"x32" right-arm module 32"x32" ottoman 32"x32" wing chair 33"x34" lounge chair 32"x32" lounge chair 30"x30" barrel chair 30"x30" headrest barrel chair 30"x29" (opens to 66") footrest

rocking chair 22"x24" arm-chair 27"x29" arm-chair 27"x27" occasional chair 23"x26" occasional chair 25"x25" occasional chair 24"x22" ottoman 30"x16" ottoman 27"x20" ottoman 22"x22"

chaise longue 60"x24" 32" round ottoman

Dining and Café Tables

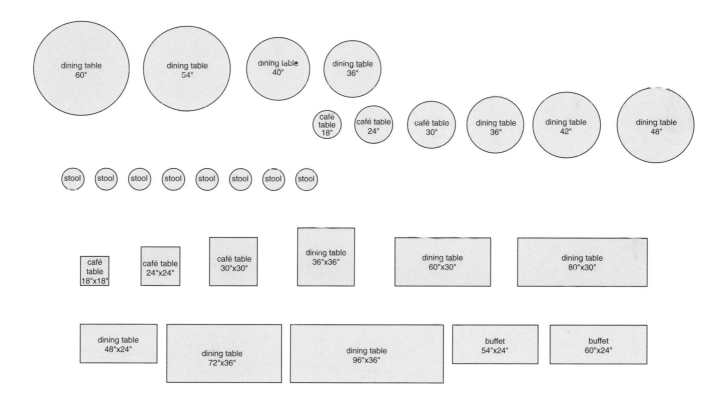

dining table 60" dining table 54" dining table 40" dining table 36" café table 18" café table 24" café table 30" dining table 36" dining table 42" dining table 48"

stool stool stool stool stool stool stool stool

café table 18"x18" café table 24"x24" café table 30"x30" dining table 36"x36" dining table 60"x30" dining table 80"x30"

dining table 48"x24" dining table 72"x36" dining table 96"x36" buffet 54"x24" buffet 60"x24"

Base Cabinets

desk 36"x24" desk 30"x24" 6"x24" base cabinet 15"x24" base cabinet 18"x24" base cabinet 21"x24" 9"x24" base cabinet 39"x24"

base cabinet 24"x24" 12"x24" base cabinet base cabinet 30"x24" base cabinet 33"x24" base cabinet 36"x24" base cabinet 18"x24"

Islands and Appliances

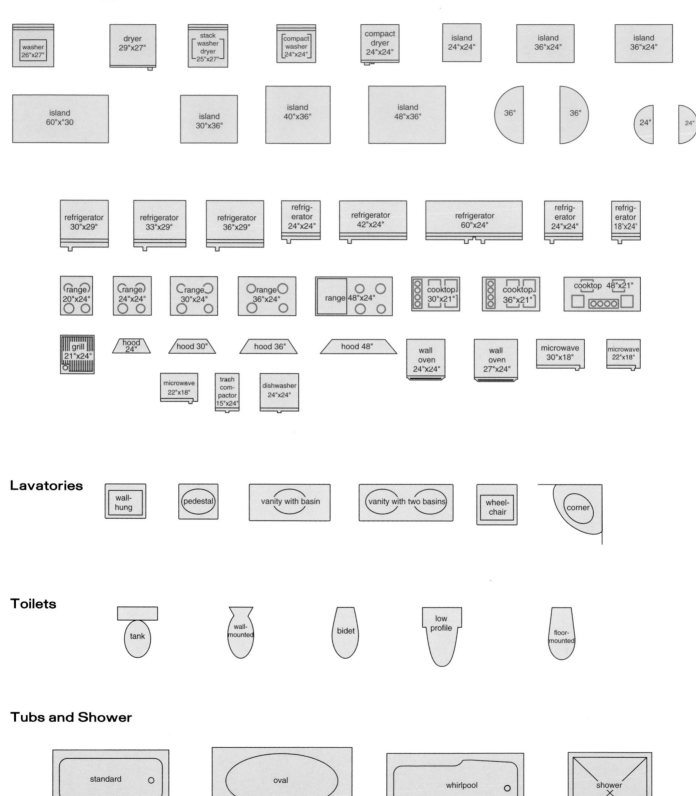

washer
26"x27"

dryer
29"x27"

stack
washer
dryer
25"x27"

compact
washer
24"x24"

compact
dryer
24"x24"

island
24"x24"

island
36"x24"

island
36"x24"

island
60"x"30

island
30"x36"

island
40"x36"

island
48"x36"

36"

36"

24"

24"

refrigerator
30"x29"

refrigerator
33"x29"

refrigerator
36"x29"

refrig-
erator
24"x24"

refrigerator
42"x24"

refrigerator
60"x24"

refrig-
erator
24"x24"

refrig-
erator
18"x24"

range
20"x24"

range
24"x24"

range
30"x24"

range
36"x24"

range 48"x24"

cooktop
30"x21"

cooktop
36"x21"

cooktop 48"x21"

grill
21"x24"

hood
24"

hood 30"

hood 36"

hood 48"

wall
oven
24"x24"

wall
oven
27"x24"

microwave
30"x18"

microwave
22"x18"

microwave
22"x18"

trash
com-
pactor
15"x24"

dishwasher
24"x24"

Lavatories

wall-
hung

pedestal

vanity with basin

vanity with two basins

wheel-
chair

corner

Toilets

tank

wall-
mounted

bidet

low
profile

floor-
mounted

Tubs and Shower

standard

oval

whirlpool

shower

Scale: 1 square=1 foot

resource guide

The following list of manufacturers and associations is meant to be a general guide to additional industry and product-related sources. It is not intended as a listing of products and manufacturers represented by the photographs in this book.

MANUFACTURERS

All Multimedia Storage
866-603-1700
www.allmultimediastorage.com
Manufactures media storage.

Amana
800-843-0304
www.amana.com
Manufactures refrigerators, dishwashers, and cooking appliances.

American Standard
www.americanstandard-us.com
Manufactures plumbing and tile products.

Andersen Windows
888-888-7020
www.andersenwindows.com
Manufactures windows and accessories.

Ann Sacks Tile & Stone, a division of Kohler
800-278-8453
www.annsacks.com
Manufactures ceramic, glass, and stone tile.

Architectural Products by Outwater
800-835-4400
www.outwater.com
Manufactures hardwood and plastic moldings, niches, frames, hardware, and other architectural products.

Archival Methods
866-877-7050
www.archivalmethods.com
Manufactures storage products.

Armstrong World Industries
717-397-0611
www.armstrong.com
Manufactures floors, cabinets, ceilings, and ceramic tiles.

Artemide
631-694 9292
www.artemide.com
Manufactures lighting fixtures.

Bach Faucets
866-863-6584
www.bachfaucet.com
Manufactures faucets.

Ballard Designs
800-536-7551
www.ballarddesigns.com
An online and catalog source for decorative accessories, including boxes and baskets.

Bassett Furniture Industries
276-629-6000
www.bassettfurniture.com
Manufactures both upholstered furniture and casegoods.

Bauer International
843-884-4007
www.bauerinternational.com
Manufactures and distributes fine furnishings.

Benjamin Moore & Co.
www.benjaminmoore.com
Manufactures paint.

Blue Mountain Wallcoverings, Inc.
866-563-9872
www.imp-wall.com

Manufactures wallcoverings under the brand names Imperial, Sunworthy, Katzenbach & Warren, and Sanitas.

Brewster Wallcovering Co.

781-963-4800

www.brewsterwallcovering.com

Manufactures wallpaper, fabrics, and borders in many patterns and styles.

Calico Corners

800-213-6366

www.calicocorners.com

A national retailer specializing in fabric. In-store services include design consultation and custom window-treatment fabrication.

California Closets

415-256-8501

www.californiaclosets.com

Manufactures closet systems.

Comfortex Window Fashions

800-843-4151

www.comfortex.com

Manufactures custom window treatments, including sheer and pleated shades, wood shutters, and blinds. Its Web site provides company information and a store locator.

Corian, a division of DuPont

800-426-7426

www.corian.com

Manufactures solid surfacing.

Country Curtains

800-456-0321

www.countrycurtains.com

A national retailer and on-line source for ready-made curtains, draperies, shades, blinds, hardware, and accessories.

Couristan, Inc.

800-223-6186

www.couristan.com

Manufactures natural and synthetic carpets and rugs.

Dex Studios

404-753-0600

www.dexstudios.com

Creates custom concrete sinks, tubs, and countertops.

Easy Closets

800-910-0129

www.easyclosets.com

Manufactures closet systems.

EGS Electrical Group

Easy Heat

860-653-1600

www.easyheat.com

Manufactures floor-warming systems.

Elfa

www.elfa.com

Manufactures storage products.

Elkay

630-574-8484

www.elkayusa.com

Manufactures sinks, faucets, and countertops.

Ethan Allen Furniture

888-324-3571

www.ethanallen.com

Manufactures upholstered furniture and casegoods.

Fisher & Paykel, Inc.

888-936-7872

www.fisherpaykel.com

Manufactures kitchen appliances.

General Electric

580-634-0151

www.ge.com

Manufactures appliances and electronics.

Ginger

www.gingerco.com

Manufactures lighting and bathroom accessories.

Glidden
800-454-3336
www.glidden.com
Manufactures 1paint.

Haier America
877-337-3639
www.haieramerica.com
Manufactures electronics and appliances, in1cluding wine cellars.

Häfele America Co.
1-800-423-3531
www.hafeleonline.com
Manufactures cabinet hardware.

Hartco Hardwood Floors
800-769-8528
www.hartcoflooring.com
Manufactures engineered-hardwood and solid-wood flooring.

Herbeau Creations of America
239-417-5368
www.herbeau.com
Makes vitreous-china fixtures.

Hoesch Design
www.hoesch.de
Manufactures tubs and shower partitions.

Hunter Douglas, Inc.
800-789-0331
www.hunterdouglas.com
Manufactures shades, blinds, and shutters. Its Web site directs consumers to designers, dealers, and installers.

Ikea
www.ikea.com
Manufactures furniture and home-organization accessories.

Jacuzzi Inc.
800-288-4002
www.jacuzzi.com
Manufactures spas and shower systems.

Jenn-Air, a division of Maytag Corp.
Maytag Customer Service

800-688-1100
www.jennair.com
Manufactures kitchen appliances.

Kirsch Window Fashions
800-538-6567
www.kirsch.com
Manufactures blinds, rods, shades, and holdbacks.

Kohler
800-456-4537
www.kohler.com
Manufactures plumbing products.

Kraftmaid Cabinetry
440-632-5333
www.kraftmaid.com
Manufactures cabinetry.

LG
800-243-0000
www.lge.com
Manufactures major appliances.

Lightology
866-954-4489
www.lightology.com
Manufactures lighting fixtures.

Manhattan Cabinetry
800-626-4288
www.manhattancabinetry.com
Manufactures Murphy beds.

Maytag Corp.
800-688-9900
www.maytag.com
Manufactures major appliances.

Merillat
www.merillat.com
Manufactures cabinets.

MGS Progetti
www.mgsprogetti.com
Manufactures stainless-steel faucets.

211

Moen
800-289-6636
www.moen.com
Manufactures plumbing products.

Motif Designs
800-431-2424
www.motif-designs.com
Manufactures fabrics and wallcoverings.

Nuheat Industries, Ltd.
800-778-WARM
www.nuheat.com
Manufactures electric radiant-floor heating systems.

NuTone, Inc.
888-336-3948
www.nutone.com
Manufactures ventilation fans, medicine cabinets, and lighting fixtures.

ORG
www.home-org.com
Manufactures home-organization products.

Organize.com
800-600-9817
www.organize.com
Sells storage and organizational tools.

OrganizedHome.com
Cynthia Townley Ewer, Editor
www.organizedhome.com
An on-line forum that offers advice to consumers about home organization.

Pittsburg Corning
800-624-2120
www.pittsburgcorning.com
Manufactures windows and glass block.

Plain and Fancy Custom Cabinetry
800-447-9006
www.plainfancycabinetry.com
Makes custom cabinetry.

Price Pfister, Inc.
800-732-8238
www.pricepfister.com
Manufactures faucets.

Robern, a div. of Kohler
www.robern.com
Manufactures medicine cabinets.

Rohm and Haas
www.rohmhaas.com
Manufactures specialty chemicals that enhance the performance of paints and coatings, computers and electronic devices, household goods, and personal-care products.

Seabrook Wallcoverings, Inc.
800-238-9152
www.seabrookwallpaper.com
Manufactures borders and wallcoverings.

Seagull Lighting Products, Inc.
856-764-0500
www.seagulllighting.com
Manufactures lighting fixtures.

Sharp
www.sharpusa.com
Manufactures consumer electronics.

Sherwin-Williams
www.sherwinwilliams.com
Manufactures paint.

Spiegel
800-474-5555
www.spiegel.com
An on-line and paper catalog source of all types of home furnishings, including window treatments, hardware, and related embellishments.

Springs Industries, Inc.
888-926-7888
www.springs.com
Manufactures window treatments, including blinds and shutters, and distributes Graber Hardware.

Thibaut Inc.
800-223-0704
www.thibautdesign.com
Manufactures wallpaper and fabrics.

Thomasville Furniture Industries
800-225-0265
www.thomasville.com
Manufactures wood and upholstered furniture and casegoods.

Toto USA
770-282-8686
www.totousa.com
Manufactures toilets, bidets, sinks, and bathtubs.

Viking Range Corp.
www.vikingrange.com
Manufactures professional-style kitchen appliances.

Villeroy and Boch
877-505-5350
www.villeroy-boch.com
Manufactures fixtures, fittings, and furniture.

Warmly Yours
800-875-5285
www.warmlyyours.com
Manufactures radiant-floor heating systems.

Whirlpool Corp.
www.whirlpool.com
Manufactures major appliances.

Wolf Appliance Company
www.wolfappliance.com
Manufactures professional-style cooking appliances.

Wood-Mode Fine Custom Cabinetry
877-635-7500
www.wood-mode.com
Manufactures custom cabinetry.

York Wallcoverings
717-846-4456
www.yorkwall.com
Manufactures borders and wallcoverings.

Stacks and Stacks
800-761-5222
www.stacksandstacks.com
Manufactures storage and organization products.

Stanley Furniture
276-627-2100
www.stanley.com
Manufactures entertainment centers and other casegoods.

Sub-Zero Freezer Co.
800-222-7820
www.subzero.com
Manufactures professional-style refrigeration appliances.

Sure-Fit, Inc.
888-754-7166
www.surefit.com
Manufactures ready-made slipcovers and pillows.

ASSOCIATIONS

American Society of Interior Designers (ASID)
202-546-3480
www.asid.org
A professional organization for designers, industry representatives, educators, and students of interior design.

National Association of Home Builders (NAHB)
800-368-5242
www.nahb.org
A trade association that helps promote the policies that make housing a national priority.

National Association of Remodeling Industry (NARI)
800-611-6274
www.nari.org
A professional organization for remodelers, contractors, and design-build professionals.

National Kitchen and Bath Association (NKBA)
800-652-2776
www.nkba.org
A national trade organization for kitchen and bath design professionals. It offers consumers product information and a referral service.

National Organization of Professional Organizers (NAPO)
847-375-4746
www.napo.net
A professional organization of consultants and manufacturers of organization products that provides referrals to the consumer.

PROFFESSIONALS

Anne Grasso
AE Grasso Spatial Design Consultants
401.273.9563
www.aegrasso.com
A space planner and interior designer based in Providence, RI.

Akemi Tanaka
akemi@akemitanaka.com
akemitanaka.com
A furniture and accessories designer.

Helene Goodman
Goodman Design Studio
732-758-9219
An interior designer based in Rumson, NJ.

Lori Jo Krengel, CKD, CBD
Kitchens by Krengel
651-698-0844
www.kitchensbykrengel.com
A kitchen and bath designer based in St. Paul, MN.

Lucianna Samu Design
luciannasamu@yahoo.com
An interior designer based in Saratoga Springs, NY.

Patricia Gaylor
Patricia Gaylor Interiors
PGaylor@PatriciaGaylor.com
www.patriciagaylor.com
An interior designer based in Little Falls, NJ.

Sunday Hendrickson
ohsunday@aol.com
An interior designer and stylist based in Los Angeles, CA.

Tracey Stephens, Allied Member ASID
Tracey Stephens Interior Design Inc.
973-744-8947
www.traceystephens.com
An interior designer based in Montclair, NJ.

glossary OF HOME DECORATING TERMS

Accent Lighting: A type of lighting that highlights an area or object to emphasize that aspect of a room's character.

Accessible Designs: Those that accommodate persons with physical disabilities.

Adaptable Designs: Those that can be easily changed to accommodate a person with disabilities.

Analogous Scheme: See "Harmonious Color Scheme."

Ambient Lighting: General illumination that surrounds a room. There is no visible source of the light.

Backlighting: Illumination coming from a source behind or at the side of an object.

Backsplash: The vertical part at the rear and sides of a countertop that protects the adjacent wall.

Box Pleat: A double pleat, underneath which the edges fold toward each other.

Built-In: Any element, such as a bookcase or cabinetry, that is built into a wall or an existing frame.

Candlepower: The luminous intensity of a beam of light (total luminous flux) in a particular direction, measured in units called candelas.

Casegoods: A piece of furniture used for storage, including cabinets, dressers, and desks.

Clearance: The amount of space between two fixtures, the centerlines of two fixtures, or a fixture and an obstacle, such as a wall.

Code: A locally or nationally enforced mandate regarding structural design, materials, plumbing, or electrical systems that state what you can or cannot do when you build or remodel.

Color Wheel: A pie-shaped diagram showing the range and relationships of pigment and dye colors.

Complementary Colors: Hues directly opposite each other on the color wheel. As the strongest contrasts, complements tend to intensify each other.

Contemporary: Any modern design (after 1920) that does not contain traditional elements.

Cove: 1. A built-in recess in a wall or ceiling that conceals an indirect light source. 2. A concave recessed molding that is usually found where the wall meets the ceiling or floor.

Daybed: A bed made up to appear as a sofa. It usually has a frame that consists of a headboard, a footboard, and a sideboard along the back.

Dimmer Switch: A switch that can vary the intensity of the light it controls.

Distressed Finish: A decorative paint technique in which the final paint coat is sanded and battered to produce an aged appearance.

Faux Finish: A decorative paint technique that imitates a pattern found in nature.

Fittings: The plumbing devices that bring water to the fixtures, such as faucets.

Fluorescent Lighting: A glass tube coated on the interior with phosphor, a chemical compound that emits light when it is activated by ultraviolet energy. Air in the tube is replaced with a combination of argon gas and a small amount of mercury.

Focal Point: The dominant element in a room or design, usually the first to catch your eye.

Footcandle: A unit that is used to measure brightness. A footcandle is equal to one lumen per square foot of surface.

Framed Cabinet: A cabinet with a full frame across the face of the cabinet box.

Frameless Cabinet: A cabinet without a face frame. It may also be called a "European-style" cabinet.

Frieze: A horizontal band at the top of the wall or just below the cornice.

Full-Spectrum Light: Light that contains the full range of wavelengths that can be found in daylight, including invisible radiation at the end of each visible spectrum.

Ground-Fault Circuit Interrupter (GFCI): A safety circuit breaker that compares the amount of current entering a receptacle with the amount leaving. If there is a discrepancy of 0.005 volt, the GFCI breaks the circuit in a fraction of a second. GFCIs are required in damp areas of the house.

Harmonious Color Scheme: Also called analogous, a combination focused on neighboring hues on the color wheel. The shared underlying color generally gives such schemes a coherent flow.

Hue: Another term for specific points on the pure, clear range of the color wheel.

Incandescent Lighting: A bulb that converts electric power into light by passing electric current through a filament of tungsten wire.

Indirect Lighting: A more subdued type of lighting that is not head-on, but rather reflected against another surface such as a ceiling.

Inlay: A decoration, usually consisting of stained wood, metal, or mother-of-pearl, that is set into the surface of an object in a pattern and finished flush.

Lambrequin: Drapery that hangs from a shelf, such as a mantel, or covering the top of a window or a door. This term is sometimes used interchangeably with valance.

Love Seat: A sofa-like piece of furniture that consists of seating for two.

Lumen: The measurement of a source's light output—the quantity of visible light.

Lumens Per Watt (LPW): The ratio of the amount of light provided to the energy (watts) used to produce the light.

Modular: Units of a standard size, such as pieces of a sofa, that can be fitted together.

Molding: An architectural band used to trim a line where materials join or create a linear decoration. It is typically made of wood, plaster, or a polymer.

Occasional Piece: A small piece of furniture for incidental use, such as end tables.

Orientation: The placement of any object or space, such as a window, a door, or a room, and its relationship to the points on a compass.

Peninsula: A countertop, with or without a base cabinet, that is connected at one end to a wall or another counter and extends outward, providing access on three sides.

Primary Color: Red, blue, or yellow that can't be produced in pig-

ments by mixing other colors. Primaries plus black and white, in turn, combine to make all the other hues.

Secondary Color: A mix of two primaries. The secondary colors are orange, green, and purple.

Sectional: Furniture made into separate pieces that coordinate with each other. The pieces can be arranged together as a large unit or independently.

Slipcover: A fabric or plastic cover that can be draped or tailored to fit over a piece of furniture.

Stud: A vertical support element made of wood or metal that is used in the construction of walls.

Task Lighting: Lighting that concentrates in specific areas for tasks, such as preparing food, applying makeup, reading, or doing crafts.

Tone: Degree of lightness or darkness of a color.

Track Lighting: Lighting that utilizes a fixed band that supplies a current to movable light fixtures.

Trompe L'oeil: Literally meaning "fool the eye," it is a painted mural in which realistic images and the illusion of three-dimensional space are created.

Tufting: The fabric of an upholstered piece or a mattress that is drawn tightly to secure the padding, creating regularly spaced indentations.

Turning: Wood that is cut on a lathe into a round object with a distinctive profile. Furniture legs, posts, and rungs are usually made in this way.

Uplight: Also used to describe the lights themselves, this is actually the term for light that is directed upward toward the ceiling.

Valance: Short drapery that hangs along the top of a window, with or without a curtain underneath.

Value: In relation to a scale of grays ranging from black to white, this is the term to describe the lightness (tints) or darkness (shades) of a color.

Vanity: a bathroom floor cabinet that usually contains a sink and storage space.

Veneer: High-quality wood that is cut into very thin sheets for use as a surface material.

Wainscotting: A wallcovering of boards, plywood, or paneling that covers the lower section of an interior wall and usually contrasts with the wall surface above.

Welt: A cord, often covered by fabric, that is used as an elegant trim on cushions, slipcovers, etc.

Work Triangle: The area bounded by the lines that connect the sink, range, and refrigerator. A kitchen may have multiple work triangles. In an ideal triangle, the distances between appliances are from 4 to 9 feet.

index

photo credits

page 1: Peter Paige, design: Helen Goodman **page 2:** Mark Lohman **page 6:** Mark Lohman **page 8:** Mark Samu **pages 10-13:** Karyn Millet **page 14:** Rob Parham Photography **page 15:** Mark Samu **page 16:** Olson Photography LLC **page 17:** Rob Parham Photography **pages 18-19:** Bjorg Magnea **page 20:** Mark Samu **page 21:** Westphalen Photography **page 22:** Mark Samu **page 23:** Olson Photography LLC **page 24:** Westphalen Photography **pages 25-27:** Mark Samu **page 28:** Karyn Millet **page 30:** Olson Photography LLC **page 31:** Bjorg Magnea **page 32:** Olson Photography LLC **pages 33-34:** Mark Samu **page 35:** *top* Mark Samu; *bottom* Westaphalen Photography **page 36:** Bjorg Magnea **page 37:** *top* Olson Photography LLC; *bottom* Westphalen Photography **page 38:** Bjorg Magnea **pages 39-40:** Olson Photography LLC **page 41:** Mark Samu **pages 42-43:** Bjorg Magnea **page 46:** Olson Photography LLC **page 48:** Tria Giovan **page 49:** Mark Samu **page 50:** Mark Lohman **page 51:** *top* Olson Photography LLC; *bottom* Mark Samu **page 53:** Mark Lohman **page 54:** *left* Mark Samu; *right* Tria Giovan **page 55:** Mark Lohman, stylist: Sunday Hendrickson **page 56:** Mark Samu **page 57:** Dan Gair Photography **pages 58-61:** Mark Samu **page 62-63:** Bjorg Magnea **pages 64-65:** Olson Photography LLC **page 66:** Mark Samu **page 68:** *top*

Minh+Wass; *bottom* Mark Samu **page 69:** Tria Giovan **page 70:** Ann Gummerson, design: Gina Fitzsimmons, Fitzsimmons Design Associates **page 71:** *top* Minh+Wass; *bottom* Olson Photography LLC **page 72:** Mark Lohman **page 73:** Beth Singer, design: Jeffrey King Interiors & Richard Ross Interiors, architect: Bryce, McCalpin & Palazzola Architects, builder: Ray Wallick **page 74:** Mark Samu **page 76-77:** melabee m miller, design: Tracey Stephens **page 78-79:** Olson Photography LLC **pages 80-81:** Bjorg Magnea **pages 82-83:** Mark Samu **pages 84,86:** Olson Photography LLC **page 87:** *top* Tria Giovan; *bottom* Olson Photography LLC **page 88:** Rob Parham Photography **page 90:** Olson Photography LLC **page 91:** Bjorg Magnea **pages 92-93:** Tria Giovan **page 95:** Bjorg Magnea **page 96:** Tria Giovan **page 97:** *top* Tria Giovan; *bottom* Rob Parham **page 98:** Tria Giovan **page 101:** *top* Tria Giovan; *bottom* Daniel Newcomb **pages 102-103:** Tria Giovan **pages 104-105:** Olson Photography LLC **pages 106-107:** Bjorg Magnea **page 108:** Olson Photography LLC **page 110:** Mark Lohman **page 112:** Eric Roth **page 114:** Tria Giovan **page 115:** Mark Samu **pages 116-123:** Mark Lohman **page 124:** Mark Samu **page 125:** *left* courtesy of Thibaut; *right* Bob Greenspan, stylist: Susan Andrews **page 126:** Mark Lohman **page 127:** courtesy of Thibaut **pages 128-129:**

Mark Lohman **pages 130-131:** Bob Greenspan, stylist: Susan Andrews **page 132:** Tria Giovan **page 135-136:** Mark Samu **page 137:** *all* Tria Giovan **pages 138-139:** Westphalen Photography **pages 140-141:** Mark Samu **page 142:** Tria Giovan **page 143:** davidduncanlivingston.com **page 144:** Bjorg Magnea **page 145:** *all* Mark Lohman **page 146:** *left* Phillip Ennis, architect: Chary & Siquenza Architects; *right* Bjorg Magnea **page 147:** Bjorg Magnea page 148-149: Tria Giovan pages 150-151: Olson Photography LLC **pages 152, 154-155:** Bjorg Magnea **page 156:** Mark Samu **page 157:** Bjorg Magnea **page 158:** *top & bottom* Bjorg Magnea; *center* Tria Giovan **pages 159-161:** Olson Photography LLC **pages 162, 164-165:** Bjorg Magnea **pages 166-167:** Mark Samu **page 168:** Tria Giovan **page 170:** Mark Lohman **pages 171-172:** Mark Samu **pages 173-174, 176-185:** Bjorg Magnea **page 186:** Tria Giovan **page 188:** Mark Lohman, stylist: Sunday Hendrickson **pages 189-195:** Tria Giovan **page 196:** Dan Gair Photography **page 197:** Mark Lohman, stylist: Sunday Hendrickson **page 198:** Tria Giovan **page 199:** *top* Mark Lohman, stylist: Sunday Hendrickson; *bottom* Tria Giovan **page 200:** Mark Lohman, stylist: Sunday Hendrickson **page 201:** Tria Giovan **pages 202-203:** Mark Lohman, stylist: Sunday Hendrickson

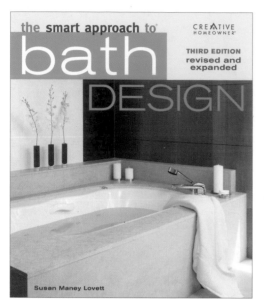
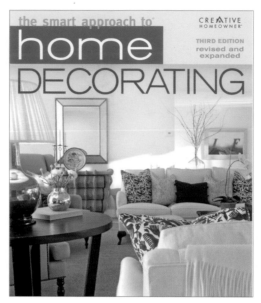